THE VEGAN HOLIDAY COOKBOOK

Festive plant-based recipes for the Christmas and Thanksgiving seasons!

Caterina Milano

© Copyright 2021 Caterina Milano - All rights reserved.

The content contained within this book may not be reproduced, duplicated or transmitted without direct written permission from the author or the publisher.

Under no circumstances will any blame or legal responsibility be held against the publisher, or author, for any damages, reparation, or monetary loss due to the information contained within this book. Either directly or indirectly. You are responsible for your own choices, actions, and results.

Legal Notice:

This book is copyright protected. This book is only for personal use. You cannot amend, distribute, sell, use, quote or paraphrase any part, or the content within this book, without the consent of the author or publisher.

Disclaimer Notice:

Please note the information contained within this document is for educational and entertainment purposes only. All effort has been executed to present accurate, up to date, and reliable, complete information. No warranties of any kind are declared or implied. Readers acknowledge that the author is not engaging in the rendering of legal, financial, medical or professional advice. The content within this book has been derived from various sources. Please consult a licensed professional before attempting any techniques outlined in this book.

By reading this document, the reader agrees that under no circumstances is the author responsible for any losses, direct or indirect, which are incurred as a result of the use of the information contained within this document, including, but not limited to, — errors, omissions, or inaccuracies.

SPECIAL BONUS!

Want this Bonus Book free?

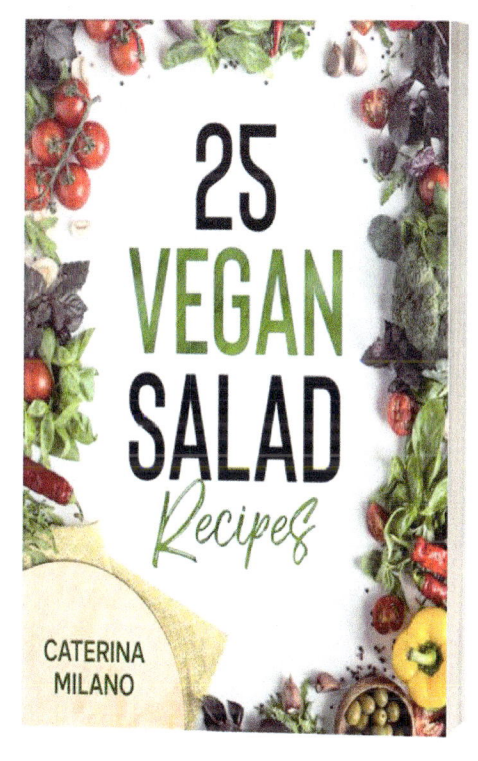

Get **FREE**, unlimited access to it and all of my new books by joining the Fan Base!

→ **SCAN WITH YOUR CAMERA TO JOIN!**

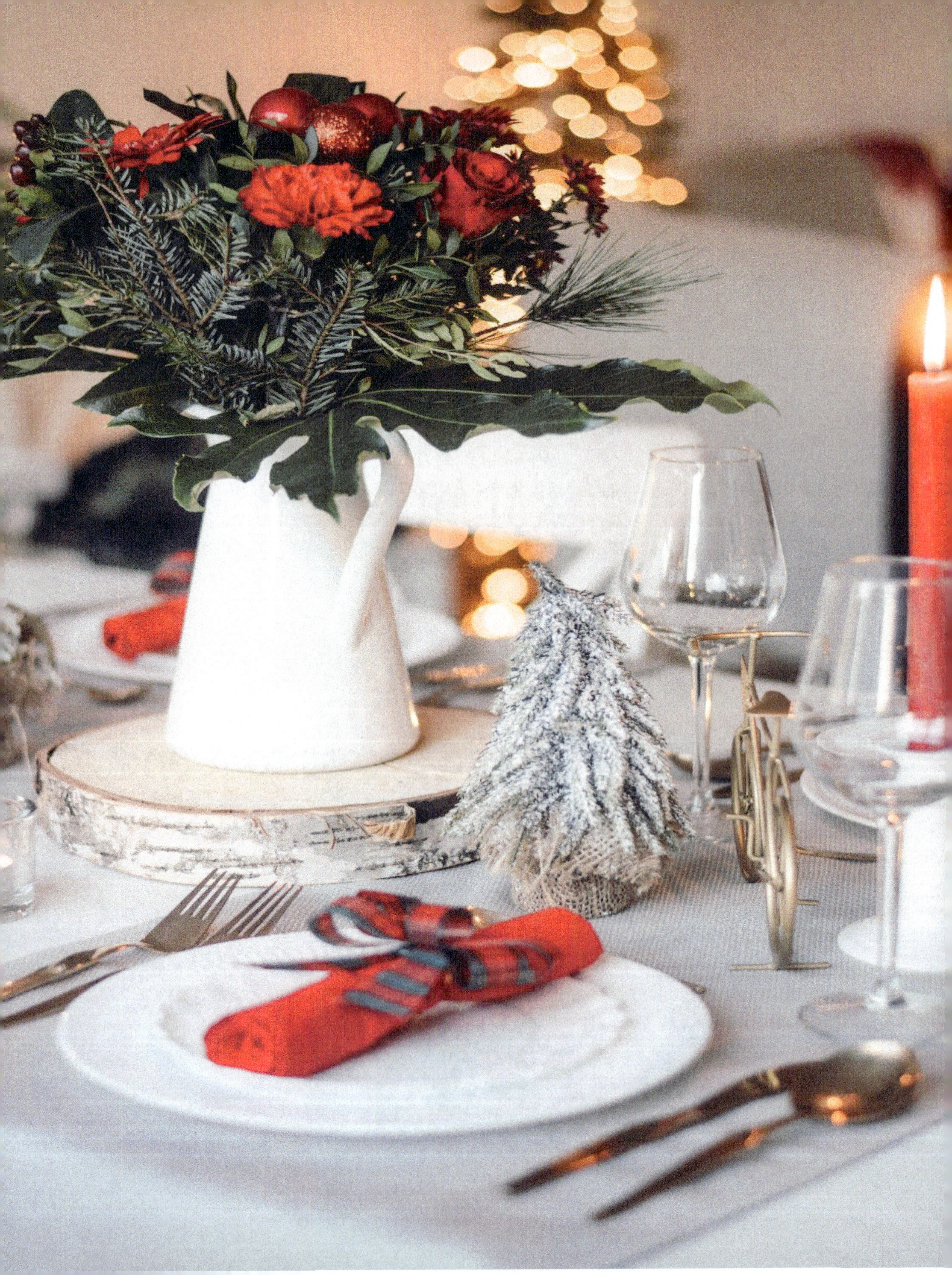

TABLE OF CONTENTS

Introduction 1

Appetizers 14

Garlic Stuffed Mushrooms 15
Indian Samosa 17
Avocado Hummus 19
Buffalo Cauliflower Wings 20
Zucchini Fritters 22

Veggie Tempura 23
Sweet Potato Latkes 25
Egg Rolls With Plum Sauce 27
Gluten Free Quinoa Mushroom Patties ... 29
Mushroom Walnut Leek Empanadas 31

Side Dishes 33

Spicy Sauteed Eggplant and Mushrooms 34
Maple Balsamic Brussels Sprouts 35
Curry Cauliflower Rice 36
Christmas Wreath Salad 37
Herb Roasted Carrots 38
Swedish Caramelized Potatoes 39

Indian Mushroom Rice Pilaf 40
Green Lentil Onion Tomato Salad 42
Maple Roasted Root Vegetables 44
Shaved Beet Chickpea Salad 45
Dressing (Stuffing) 46
Mashed Potatoes and Gravy 48

Main Dishes 50

Quinoa Lentil Nut Meatloaf 51
Veggie Pot Pie 53
Roasted Cauliflower Steaks 55

Shepherd's Pie 56
Spinach Basil Trottole With Pesto Sauce . 58
Roasted Cabbage Steaks 60

Spiced Chickpea Stuffed Sweet Potatoes 61	Peanut Spinach Pesto Gnocchi 68
Warm Green Pea Broccoli Pasta 62	White Spinach Mushroom Pinenut Lasagna 69
Indian Lentil Daal Curry 63	Potato Pear Casserole 72
Mushroom Stuffed Cabbage Rolls 65	Butternut Squash Cranberry Wellington 73
Tomato Bean Carrot Stew 67	

Desserts 75

Pear Walnut Cake 76	Vanilla Mocha Cheesecake 92
Lemon Coconut Cookies 78	Christmas Fruit Cake 94
Dark Chocolate Strawberry Cake 80	Cranberry Pistachio White Chocolate Bark 96
Peppermint Cupcakes 82	Peppermint Ice Cream 97
Carrot Cake 84	Gingerbread Ice Cream 98
Chocolate Orange Truffles 86	Peppermint Berry Chocolate Bark 99
Matcha Madeleines 87	Pumpkin Pie 100
Cranberry Almond Pound Cake 89	
Chocolate Crinkle Cookies 91	

Conclusion 102

INTRODUCTION

When the air is crisp, and it's just beginning to feel like winter, you know Thanksgiving is around the corner, and Christmas is also not too far behind. It's a time to reflect on all that we have to be thankful for - our health, family, friends, home, and food. Whether you're hosting a family gathering or attending someone else's celebration, bringing joy to your holiday table is always the aim.

As vegans, we all know how challenging it is to attend a holiday party hosted by individuals who are not vegan. Most times, we are limited to munching on the side dishes. However, this problem can easily be resolved if you host the dinner! You can plan your own menu featuring vegan dishes and show your friends and family that being a vegan is not so boring. From vegan cheesecake to mushroom spinach pine nut lasagna to Indian samosas and curried cauliflower rice. This vegan cookbook will allow you to show off your new cooking skills. Alternatively, if you are not up for hosting Christmas dinner, cook 1 or 2 vegan dishes and bring them to the party. This way, you can be sure the food you are consuming is 100% vegan, and the host will not have to alter their menu to make new dishes.

Being vegan can be difficult in the holiday season. Many traditional Thanksgiving and Christmas recipes are based on animal products such as butter, cream, or meat. This can make vegan cooking difficult as many common ingredients contain animal products. This cookbook offers an alternative to those looking for a vegetarian-friendly but still delicious dish perfect for the holiday season.

Whether you are hosting the dinner or bringing a few dishes to a potluck Holiday dinner, this cookbook provides you with a diverse range of vegan recipes to ensure you will never be hungry during the holidays again. These vegan dishes are so good that no one will miss the ham, turkey, eggs, milk, or butter. In fact, you'll probably need to double these recipes because they are so flavorful and delicious; before you know it, all of your food will be gone.

The best way to avoid the craziness of vegan holidays is with a little preparation. When it comes to cooking a vegan Christmas or Thanksgiving dinner, practice is extremely important. If you want to have a successful dinner party, then plan ahead. Figure out if you are hosting the dinner, decide whom you are inviting, plan a menu that fits all of your guest's needs. This will help you eliminate the last-minute stress that can happen as a result of poor planning. Luckily your job is halfway done as you now have over 50 vegan holiday recipes to choose from. The most challenging part of planning your vegan feast is choosing which recipes you want to prepare for your dinner. Whether you're looking to make something new or a tried-and-true family favorite, we've got you covered.

But first, we will talk about veganism and why vegan holidays? We will shed some light on the benefits of veganism and why you should consider it for sustainable living. Further along, there are some tips and tricks for making your festive vegan meals perfect for the holiday season.

Benefits of Veganism

The world is changing rapidly, we are slowly being forced to become greener, more sustainable and to leave a smaller footprint in the world.

Eating vegan reduces your carbon footprint, making it a more sustainable option than one with meat. It takes around 15,500 liters of water to produce 1 kilo of beef, and almost 70 percent (or four-fifths) of all agricultural land is used for farming livestock.

So much space is needed to provide sustenance for those who eat animal products - an estimated 8 billion people worldwide. So, you can see why it would be advantageous if everyone went veggie or cut down on their consumption habits considerably.

The United Nations stated that by changing our diets, we have an opportunity for improved health and environmental sustainability because processed foods often require fossil fuels during production, which contribute heavily to climate change. According to the UN, the best thing people can do is eat less meat and get their protein from other sources such as beans, legumes, or eggs.

Here is some data to showcase what veganism can save:

- 20.4 kilograms of grains per day
- Four thousand two hundred liters of water per day.
- 2.8 meters squared of forested land per day.
- 9.1 kilograms CO2 equivalent per day.

To sum it up, we all have the potential to make a difference in this world, one person at a time. When you eat animal products, your decision to do so has an impact on the environment. People need to understand the impact of what kind of food we consume and how much waste will occur after consumption.

Health Benefits of Veganism

For those looking for a way to improve their health and wellness, veganism is perfect. It can help lower cholesterol, reduce the risk of cancer, diabetes, and heart disease-all while preventing animal cruelty. And that is not all; even the cost of eating vegan is way less than other diets.

Nevertheless, there are many more reasons to stay on a vegan lifestyle.

A vegan diet is rich in nutrients

A vegan diet is a healthy and compassionate way to live. Those who follow this eating style enjoy consuming more fiber, antioxidants, energy-boosting nutrients like beta-carotene or vitamin C than those without it; these are just two among many other benefits you can reap from eating from the plant kingdom.

A vegetarian lifestyle with no meat but plenty of fruits, vegetables, etc. offers your body everything needed for optimal health while also being kinder on Mother Earth. Plant products lead to a greater yield per acre, leading to sustainable agriculture practices.

Minimizes the danger of cancer and other deadly diseases
In a recent study, plant-based foods were found to have powerful antioxidants that can protect us from diseases. Vegans are found to have higher concentrations of carotenoids and lower levels of saturated fatty acids when compared with non-vegetarians or meat-eaters. This means they are less likely to get sick than those who don't follow this lifestyle choice.

Boosts mood
It turns out that when you avoid eating meat, your conscience stays clear. Studies show that vegans and vegetarians might be happier than those who eat fish or flesh foods. This is true for mental health benefits as well. Those who consume vegan products have an easier time coping with daily tasks while feeling more fulfilled at home as well. They often report better moods throughout their days than omnivores or even strict dieters.

Maintains a healthy body weight
Vegan foods are healthy and tasty, but they also tend to be lower in calories than animal-derived ones. The most common vegan dishes contain significantly less saturated fat than meats do. Many studies have shown that vegans can maintain body weight without actively cutting calories while enjoying delicious food. A new study has found that vegans have a lower body mass index (BMI) than people who eat animal-based products.

A vegan diet is skin-friendly
Some people think that achieving a glowing complexion means they need to avoid dairy, but the truth is it's not just dairy that needs to be avoided. The more fruits and veggies you eat in your everyday life - even if it's just salad with dairy-free dressing for dinner every night will help keep your skin healthy. It provides essential vitamins necessary for clear skin, such as antioxidants and vitamin C.

Can help alleviate arthritis pain
Consuming animal-derived foods has been linked with pain and inflammation. The logical argument for eating a vegan diet is that it can help reduce the symptoms of arthritis. Probiotic plant-based foods such as fermented vegetables may also benefit your large intestine by boosting good bacteria. This, in turn, increases nutrient absorption rates while reducing discomfort in other areas like the stomach or joints.

Prevents Type 2 Diabetes

When you have diabetes, cutting out meat and dairy products can have many benefits. But what about when the carbs in bread aren't enough? Eating vegan might just help reduce your risk of developing diabetes by up 78%. Plus, high fiber plants keep blood sugar levels stable so that even if there's a spike or dip, they won't affect Type 2 Diabetes.

Improves cholesterol levels

Cholesterol is an essential substance that helps the body produce cell walls. When cholesterol levels are too high, it can result in fatty deposits on blood vessels, restricting their flow and leading to heart attack or stroke. However-a healthy diet filled with plant-based foods has been shown to reduce LDL ('bad' Cholesterols by 10% -15%). For people following strict vegan diets, there have even been findings showing how much lower these figures could potentially go down to reducing LDL by around 30%.

Lowers blood pressure

Your diet can make a huge difference when it comes to your health. That's why Physicians Committee for Responsible Medicine recommends that you consume more plant-based foods and fewer animal products, such as meat or dairy products. The latter may increase blood pressure levels in some people, according to several studies performed over time.

The researchers analyzed data from 39 studies and found that people who follow vegetarian diets have lower blood pressure than those following an omnivore diet. The article published in JAMA Internal Medicine explored the health benefits of plant-based foods for our bodies, specifically prevention of high blood pressure.

It keeps the brain strong

With so many health benefits to a plant-based diet, it is no wonder that there are mental ones too. Feller says, "there's compelling research examining plant-based diets and their role in slowing the progression of Alzheimer's." A review from Frontiers in Aging Neuroscience found just one extra hundred grams per day (about half a cup) of plant-based food could reduce your risk by 13%.

Helps you live longer

A plant-based diet may be the answer to an extended life span. The Journal of American Heart Association study found that people who eat meatless meals live 25% longer than others. In a study published in April 2018, The Journal of Nutrition discovered that healthy plant-based foods extended our body's protection by another 5%.

One of the main reasons why people choose a vegan lifestyle is because they believe that by avoiding these products, they're doing something good for themselves and others around them. Many vegans see this as a way of being, and we couldn't agree more.

Go vegan (for the animals)

To prevent further environmental damage, eliminate animal products in your diet. The cessation of animal agriculture will have a significant effect on the environment. It causes air and water pollution by producing more than 20 Gigatonnes (Gt) worth of waste every year which encourages deforestation contributing significantly towards climate change when not correctly disposed of.

Tips for hosting dinner with Non-Vegan guests

Whether you are an experienced vegan or a new vegan, the holidays can be as challenging as trying to explain the concept of veganism to an avid meat lover. Sometimes dealing with non-vegan friends and family or trying to plan a vegan Christmas or Thanksgiving menu can be stressful. However, these negative feelings can easily be avoided with a little preparation.

If your friends and family are vegan, then the sky's the limit. They will be more open-minded about trying new vegan dishes. You'll have no problem whipping up some new recipes from this book with delicious fruits and vegetables.

When you invite a non-vegan to your home, make sure you do the following for them:

Respect their choices
As the popular proverb goes, "Live and let live." Well, that's exactly how it should be. We all have different lifestyles, but at the end of the day, we just want respect for ourselves as people living their lives to the fullest potential. And this should be without someone trying to tell them otherwise or talking down to you because your choices don't align with theirs.

Know your guests
If you are unsure what to serve when it comes time to plan the menu, ask the guests! They may have some great suggestions. Many people also have diverse dietary needs, gluten-free, nut allergies, etc.. so it's a good idea to know ahead of time.

Larger portions, more courses
The vegan diet is always less calorie-dense than meat and cheese. Make sure you have plenty of dishes available to fill up all your guests.

Get vegan foods they eat onto the table
You can always rely on a good dip for your appetizers! Hummus or olive tapenade (homemade) are all great alternatives. There's a ton of great vegan food out there that doesn't need replacements such as baguettes & roasted garlic, green beans, cranberries, sauerkraut, succotash, sweet potato casserole, apple crumble, butternut squash soup, hot apple cider. Everyone loves chips and salsa or try serving up some guacamole too. Go above and beyond with your food to impress guests by making it fresh from scratch.

Be adventurous, try new recipes, or make classic dishes in a different way. You can even change up the ingredients for everyday favorites like guacamole. Don't settle on store-bought dip when you know how easy it is to whip up some tasty homemade hummus instead. Add plenty of garlic cloves into olive oil before blending them until they turn brown, then add salt & pepper as desired.

Do not utter the word "vegan"
Try to conduct the meal as if it is completely normal and ordinary. The mind is a powerful thing. Try not to say, "the food is vegan." It can alter someone's thoughts, and sometimes it can make one think the food is not tasty enough to enjoy anymore. Be a little creative. For instance, make vegan macaroni & cheese casserole that will fool any meat eater.

The best way to promote your vegan food is not with words but through actions. You'll need some patience and creativity because no one wants a bland meal. But when they taste something so good and appreciate it, your efforts are worth every minute.

Conversations with Non-Vegans

Talking around the dinner table is a staple of holiday tradition. One of the most challenging aspects of vegan living is how to handle conversations with non-vegans. Although this may seem simple, it can be quite complex, and there are many ways that you can approach this topic. So, don't get flustered when you find yourself in a conversation about why you don't eat meat or use animal products anymore.

Here's what to do:

Stay calm and collected
Avoid getting defensive if someone questions your choices. Be open about your lifestyle without being pushy or preachy. If they ask, tell them what made you go vegan but also emphasize that it's not for everyone because we're all different. No one should feel pressured into doing something they are uncomfortable with.

Do not take anything personally
Answer questions about veganism as if it were just one more option in a long list of lifestyle choices. Use phrases like "I love to try new things..," or mention that being vegan isn't for everyone because other factors are at play besides diet preferences. When you have someone close who disagrees with your decision, never take their opinion too seriously.

Do not boast
The vegan diet is portrayed as the perfect solution to all of our health problems. The truth is that lifestyle choices are complex when it comes to weight loss or disease prevention. Both can fail if you don't watch what's going into your body (not enough calories/nutrients/exercise).

Practice. Practice. Practice.
You might find yourself answering questions in ways you wish you didn't. These might get you emotional or angry sometimes. This is especially true when family members

who know how to push your buttons try their best. But with each talk about these issues, you'll get better at answering questions. Practice makes perfect, as humans we are imperfect beings after all.

Lead by example
How can one not get gripped in an argument about diet? The Paleo versus vegan debate has been going on for ages, and no matter how hard you try to stay objective, there are just too many emotions involved. The only way to persuade others to adopt your diet is by being the best and healthiest vegan you can be. If people see that it works for you, they might copy the kind of food or exercise routine you use.

Do not lose your 'positive' spirit
Being vegan can be like being on an island. You feel so different from your non-vegan peers and friends that it's hard to explain. However, the positives outweigh any negative feelings you might have about this lifestyle decision. People who indulge in animal products may seem intimidating when they encounter a vegan for the first time. After realizing what we eat isn't just salads all day long, you might be able to have a conversation about food.

Know when to walk away
You can't convince everyone, and some people get defensive at the mere presence of a vegan. Let them know that you are happy to have an honest conversation about why they eat meat-heavy diets (or even defend their positions) because it will only help both parties to come to terms with our differences in lifestyle choices. Excuse yourself to go do something important in the kitchen.

Accept them
People are complex creatures. While we can't force them to change overnight or at all, sometimes it takes years before someone decides to try something new in life. But the conversation will be better if you remove any expectations for how long their response might take. All that's left then is just providing people with information so that when they're ready to make an informed decision on this journey called "life".

Change the subject

The best way to handle difficult talks about veganism with non-vegans is by changing the subject. Talk about other things than just food and what people eat or don't eat in general! After all, there are so many more important aspects of life other than our dietary preferences - remember that next time an argument breaks out over something as simple as food, shift the conversation to something serious such as current events or world news.

Basic food substitutions

What do vegans eat at Holiday dinners?" You can still have all your favorites! Stuffing (made in a pan), cranberry sauce, vegan gravy and mashed potatoes. All you need to do is replace the turkey with some fantastic Main Course outlined in the book. Most Holiday classics are not vegan, luckily you can experiment with flavors ahead of time. Purchase vegan ingredients you've never tried, add new spices and test out new recipes before your big dinner. Let this cookbook serve as a guide. There are at least a few dishes in this book, such as Indian mushroom rice pilaf and caramelized potatoes you may not have tried before. So get experimenting! By the time Thanksgiving or Christmas rolls around, you will have an arsenal of vegan recipes to prepare for your feast!

Most classic Holiday meals can be veganized, for example, holiday meatloaves can be made from nuts such as walnuts and pecans or legumes such as beans and lentils. You can make side dishes from vegetables and legumes; simply omit the cheese, butter, or dairy products. In addition to this, there are vegan alternatives available such as nutritional yeast and vegan butter. Most vegan desserts and cookies resemble their animal-product counterparts. However, be sure to avoid dairy products. You can also substitute ground flax seeds for eggs in most recipes.

You might not have thought about it, but a lot of the little things you do can make something vegan-friendly. The following vegan substitutes are an option.

Cheese is an essential ingredient for many dishes, but vegans can do without it. There are some great vegan cheese alternatives out there that will give your food the same consistency and taste as regular mozzarella sticks or lasagna noodles. If your family is not into plant-based foods and you want them on board with a dish, serve cheese side dishes so they can enjoy it too.

You can make your favorite recipe vegan without milk? It's actually quite simple. All you need is some soy or almond milk alternatives and voila. You can enjoy all those sugary beverages like chocolate mocha latte while sticking with the healthiest diet ever.

Cut the butter and switch it out for something vegan-friendly. Olive oil or vegan butter work great.

Some examples of substitutes are listed in the table.

There are many vegan substitutes that can be used in place of animal products to make your favorite dishes. Here is a list of the most popular vegan substitutions.

Animal-based food	Substitute
Animal milk	Soy/almond/coconut /rice milk
Butter	Safflower, olive, sunflower or grapeseed oil, Earth Balance butter
Meat	Tofu/mushrooms/Numerous Main courses
Eggs	Chickpea flour/banana
Cottage cheese	Tofu/vegan cottage cheese
Dairy cream	Cashew/almond paste/vegan creamer
Milk yogurt	Coconut or nut yogurt
Whipped cream	Coconut Whipped cream
Honey	Agave nectar, maple syrup

Adopting a vegan lifestyle can leave you yearning for items such as chocolate and cheese, especially over the holidays. Most Holiday menus feature fancy charcuterie boards filled with salami, cheese, fruits, as well as boxes of chocolate that act as the precursor to the main meal. However, there is a simple way to avoid temptation. Unlike our vegan ancestors, who had to deal with the disappointment of not being able to indulge in these non-vegan items, there are several types of vegan cheeses and chocolates available on the market. Purchase plenty of your favorite vegan snacks to get you through the holiday season.

With the holiday season upon us, we know that it can be hard to find time for cooking and entertaining. With the season of giving and we hope you'll give some thought to what your loved ones might like on their table this year. This festive plant-based recipes book is a great survival guide for the Christmas and Thanksgiving Seasons: This time of year is a great opportunity to make your favorite dishes with plant-based ingredients For those who are not vegan or vegetarian, this may be an excellent way to introduce more vegetables into your diet in order to live a healthier lifestyle.

APPETIZERS

- Garlic Stuffed Mushrooms
- Indian Samosas
- Avocado Hummus
- Buffalo Cauliflower Wings
- Zucchini Fritters
- Veggie Tempura
- Sweet Potato Latkes
- Egg Rolls with Plum Sauce
- Gluten-Free Quinoa Mushroom Patties
- Mushroom Walnut Leek Empanadas

GARLIC STUFFED MUSHROOMS

These garlic stuffed mushrooms are the perfect appetizer. Filled with vegan mozzarella cheese, onions, shallots, bell peppers, and bread crumbs and baked to perfection, these stuffed mushrooms are filled with flavor.

Prep Time: 20 minutes| Cook Time: 20 minutes|
Total Time: 40 minutes| Servings: 20

Ingredients

- 20 button mushrooms, cleaned, stems removed (reserve the stems)
- 2 tablespoons (30 ml) olive oil
- 2 shallots, minced
- ¼ yellow bell pepper, minced
- 2 cloves garlic, minced
- 1 teaspoon (5 ml) salt
- ½ teaspoon (2.5 ml) black pepper
- ½ cup (120 ml) shredded vegan mozzarella cheese
- 1 cup (235 ml) panko breadcrumbs
- 1 teaspoon (5 ml) Italian seasoning

Instructions

1. Turn your oven to 350°F (175°C).
2. Finely chop the reserved button mushrooms stems and set them aside.
3. Place the olive oil in a frying pan and set it over medium high-heat.
4. Add the shallots and bell pepper and saute for 2-3 minutes until the shallots are translucent.
5. Next, add the minced garlic and cook for 1 minute until fragrant, then add the mushroom stems and cook them for another 2-3 minutes.
6. Add the bread crumbs and Italian seasoning to the mushroom mixture and cook it for 2-3 minutes, constantly stirring until toasted.
7. Stir in the mozzarella cheese and set the garlic filling aside.

8. Arrange the button mushroom onto a parchment-lined cookie sheet and stuff each mushroom with the garlic filling.
9. Bake the garlic stuffed mushrooms for 20-25 minutes until golden.
10. Serve and enjoy!

INDIAN SAMOSA

This traditional Indian dish features crispy, flaky dough and a curry-flavored potato, pea, and carrot filling that's fried to golden brown perfection. Get ready for these samosas to disappear because they are simply that delicious.

Prep Time: 20 minutes| Cook Time: 45 minutes|
Total Time: 1 hour 5 minutes| Servings: 13

Ingredients

For the samosa dough:

- 2 cups (470 ml) all-purpose flour
- ¼ cup (60 ml) vegetable oil
- ¾ teaspoon (4 ml) salt
- 6 tablespoons (90 ml) water

For the samosa filling:

- 5 medium potatoes
- 1 tablespoon (15 ml) olive oil
- 2 cloves garlic, minced
- 1 teaspoon (5 ml) ginger, grated
- 1 teaspoon (5 ml) ground cumin
- ½ teaspoon (2.5 ml) turmeric
- 1 tablespoon (15 ml) garam masala
- 1 teaspoon (5 ml) salt to taste
- ¼ cup (60 ml) frozen peas
- ¼ cup (60 ml) frozen carrots
- 2 cups (470 ml) vegetable oil for deep frying

Instructions

1. To make the samosa dough, whisk the flour and salt in a bowl, then add the oil and rub it into the flour salt mixture until it has pea-sized clumps.
2. Beginning with 4 tablespoons of water, add the water to the flour oil mixture and mix until a firm, stiff dough forms adding more water if necessary.
3. Cover the samosa dough with plastic wrap and let sit for 25-30 minutes.
4. To make the samosa filling, boil the potatoes until they are tender, then set them aside to cool completely.

5. Peel the potatoes and crumble the potatoes into smaller pieces, and set them aside. Do not mash the potatoes.
6. Add the tablespoon of olive oil to a skillet and set it over medium-high heat.
7. Add the garlic, ginger, cumin, turmeric, garam masala, and salt and cook it for 1 minute until fragrant.
8. Add the crumbled potatoes and stir to coat the potatoes in the seasoning.
9. Add the peas and carrots and saute for 2-3 minutes, then remove the filling from the stove and let it cool slightly.
10. To assemble the samosas, divide the dough into 13 even portions.
11. Flatten each ball and roll into a 3-inch circle.
12. Coat the edges of the samosa dough with water and add 1-2 tablespoons of the samosa filling to one half of the samosa dough, leaving a ½-inch border.
13. Fold the free edge of the dough over the samosa filling and pinch and fold the edges of the dough to seal the samosa.
14. To fry the samosas, place the vegetable oil into a deep skillet and set it over medium-high heat.
15. Once the oil has a temperature of 300°F (150°C), lower 3-4 samosas into the oil and fry the samosas for 3-4 minutes per side until golden brown.
16. Drain the samosas on a paper towel-lined plate.
17. Serve and enjoy!

AVOCADO HUMMUS

This twist on classic hummus features creamy avocados, zesty lemon juice, and tahini. This avocado hummus is ultra creamy and delicious. Serve with pita or tortilla chips for best results.

Prep Time: 10 minutes| Total Time: 10 minutes| Servings: 4

Instructions

- 1 15 oz. (445 ml) can chickpeas
- ¼ cup (60 ml) lemon juice
- 2 tablespoons (30 ml) tahini
- 2 garlic cloves
- ¾ teaspoon (4 ml) salt
- 2 small avocados halved, pitted, and scooped out of the peel
- 1 teaspoon (5 ml) paprika

Instructions

1. Add the chickpeas to a bowl of water and rub them together to remove the skins, then drain the chickpeas and place them into a food processor's bowl.
2. Process the chickpeas until they resemble a powder, then add the lemon juices, tahini, garlic, and salt and blend for 3-5 minutes until the hummus is smooth and creamy.
3. Next, add the avocados and blend the hummus until smooth and creamy.
4. Place the avocado hummus into a serving bowl, and smooth it into an even layer.
5. Make an impression in the avocado hummus with the back of a spoon and add more olive oil, top with a few chickpeas if desired, and sprinkle the paprika on top.
6. Serve and enjoy!

BUFFALO CAULIFLOWER WINGS

Believe it or not, these buffalo cauliflower wings are baked, not fried. With delicious fried flavor, these buffalo cauliflower wings are a great way to spice up your Christmas menu.

Prep Time: 10 minutes| Cook Time: 25 minutes|
Total Time: 35 minutes| Servings: 6

Ingredients

For the cauliflower:

- 1 head cauliflower, cut into florets
- 1 teaspoon (5 ml) salt
- 1 teaspoon (5 ml) garlic powder
- 1 teaspoon (5 ml) onion powder
- 1 teaspoon (5 ml) smoked paprika
- ¾ teaspoon (4 ml) cayenne pepper
- ¾ cup (175 ml) almond milk

For the buffalo sauce:

- ½ cup (120 ml) buffalo wing sauce
- 3 tablespoons (45 ml) salted butter
- 1 teaspoon (5 ml) garlic powder
- 2 tablespoons (30 ml) agave nectar

Instructions

1. Turn your oven to 450°F (232°C), then spray a cookie sheet with non-stick spray.
2. Whisk the salt, garlic powder, onion powder, paprika, cayenne powder, and almond milk in a bowl.
3. Dredge the cauliflower florets into the seasoned milk, allowing the excess almond milk to drop off, then place them in an even layer onto the prepared cookie sheet.
4. Bake the cauliflower florets for 10 minutes, then turn them over and bake for an additional 10 minutes.
5. To make the buffalo wing sauce, whisk the buffalo wing sauce, butter, garlic powder, and agave nectar in a medium saucepan and place it over a medium-high flame.

6. Once the buffalo wing sauce comes to a boil, cook it for 2-3 minutes, then remove from the stove.
7. Brush the cauliflower wings with the buffalo wing sauce and bake for 7 minutes.
8. Switch your oven to the broil function and cook the cauliflower wings for 2-3 minutes.
9. Serve and enjoy!

ZUCCHINI FRITTERS

These zucchini fritters are light with a crispy exterior and a tender interior. Made with a few simple ingredients, this appetizer takes less than 30 minutes, which means you'll have more time to focus on preparing your main dishes.

Prep Time: 15 minutes| Cook Time: 10 minutes|
Total Time: 25 minutes| Servings: 4

Ingredients

- 3 large zucchini, trimmed, shredded
- 1 teaspoon (5 ml) salt
- 2 tablespoons (30 ml) ground flaxseeds
- 5 tablespoons (75 ml) water
- ½ cup (120 ml) all-purpose flour
- ¼ cup (60 ml) tapioca starch
- 1 teaspoon (5 ml) baking powder
- 1 shallot, minced
- 2 garlic cloves, minced
- 2 tablespoons (30 ml) olive oil

Instructions

1. Add the shredded zucchini into a colander set in the sink, add the salt, toss to combine, and let it sit for 10 minutes.
2. Combine the flaxseeds and water in a bowl and set it aside for 5 minutes.
3. Squeeze all of the as much of the moisture from the zucchini as you can and add it to the flaxseeds.
4. Add the all-purpose flour, tapioca starch, baking powder, shallots, and garlic and mix until thoroughly combined.
5. Place the olive oil into a non-stick skillet and set it over medium.
6. Scoop 2 tablespoons of the zucchini into the skillet and flatten the fritters with the back of the spoon.
7. Cook the zucchini fritters for 2-3 minutes per side until golden, then drain them on a paper towel-lined plate.
8. Serve and enjoy!

VEGGIE TEMPURA

Fresh vegetables are coated in a tempura batter, then fried to perfection. Serve alongside a flavorful sauce made of tamari, coconut aminos, mirin, and maple syrup; this is seriously a delicious appetizer!

Prep Time: 10 minutes| Cook Time: 25 minutes|
Total Time: 35 minutes| Servings: 6

Ingredients

For the veggie tempura:

- 1 cup (235 ml) all-purpose flour
- 2 tablespoons (30 ml) cornstarch
- 1 tablespoon (15 ml) baking powder
- ½ teaspoon (2.5 ml) salt
- 1 teaspoon (5 ml) garlic powder
- 1 teaspoon (5 ml) ground thyme
- 1 cup (235 ml) sparkling water
- 2 cups (470 ml) oil, for frying
- ½ large head of broccoli, cut into florets
- ½ large head of cauliflower, cut into florets
- 1 onion, cut into ½-inch slices
- 1 bunch asparagus, cut into spears

For the mirin sauce:

- 1 cup (235 ml) water
- 2 tablespoons (30 ml) tamari
- 2 tablespoons (30 ml) coconut aminos
- ¼ cup (60 ml) mirin
- 2 tablespoons (30 ml) maple syrup

Instructions

1. Place the oil into a deep skillet and set it over medium-high heat.
2. To make the tempura batter, whisk the all-purpose flour, baking powder, salt, garlic powder, and ground thyme in a bowl.
3. Add the sparkling water and whisk just until combined.

4. Dredge the vegetables into the tempura batter, making sure to allow the excess batter to drop off.
5. Once the oil has a temperature of 350°F (175°C), place the vegetables into the oil and cook them for 1-2 minutes per side.
6. Drain the tempura vegetables onto a wire rack set over a cookie sheet.
7. To make the mirin sauce, add the tamari, coconut aminos, mirin, and maple syrup to a saucepan, set it over medium-high, and allow it to boil.
8. Decrease the flame to medium-low and let cook for 5 minutes.
9. Pour the mirin sauce into a serving dish and serve along with the tempura veggies.
10. Serve and enjoy!

SWEET POTATO LATKES

These sweet potato latkes are a modern twist on traditional Jewish latkes. Bursting with flavor, and crispy on the outside and tender on the inside, these latkes are the ideal holiday appetizer.

Prep Time: 20 minutes| Cook Time: 8 minutes|
Total Time: 28 minutes| Servings: 6

Ingredients

- 2 tablespoons (30 ml) ground flaxseed meal
- 3 tablespoons (45 ml) water
- 3 medium sweet potatoes, cut into wedges
- 1 medium red onion, roughly chopped
- 1 tablespoon (5 ml) garlic paste
- ½ cup (120 ml) of all-purpose flour
- 1 teaspoon (5 ml) salt
- 1 teaspoon (5 ml) black pepper
- ½ teaspoon (2.5 ml) smoked paprika
- 1 teaspoon (5 ml) ground thyme
- 4 tablespoons (60 ml) canola oil

Instructions

1. Whisk the flaxseed meal and water in a bowl, then set aside for 5 minutes.
2. Grate the sweet potatoes and red onion using a food processor outfitted with the grating blade.
3. Place the sweet potato and onion mixture onto a clean kitchen towel, squeeze as much water from the sweet potato mixture as possible, and then place it into a bowl.
4. Add the flaxseed mixture, garlic paste, all-purpose flour, salt, pepper, smoked paprika, and thyme, and mix well.
5. Place the olive oil into a frying pan and set over medium-high heat.
6. Scoop 2 tablespoons of the sweet potato latke batter into your hands, flatten it into a pancake, then place it into the skillet.

7. Cook the sweet potato latkes for 3-4 minutes per side until golden, then drain them on a paper towel-lined plate.
8. Garnish the sweet potato latkes with vegan sour cream and smoked paprika.
9. Serve and enjoy!

EGG ROLLS WITH PLUM SAUCE

Whether you bake or fry these egg rolls, they will be absolutely delicious. Served with a delightful, flavorful plum sauce, get ready for a round of applause.

Prep Time: 10 minutes| Cook Time: 20 minutes|
Total Time: 30 minutes| Servings: 18

Ingredients

For the plum sauce:

- 1 cup (235 ml) plum jam
- 1 tablespoon (30 ml) apple cider vinegar
- 1 teaspoon (5 ml) garlic powder
- ½ teaspoon (2.5 ml) ground ginger
- ¼ teaspoon (1 ml) allspice
- 1 teaspoon (5 ml) soy sauce
- ½ cup (120 ml) water

For the egg rolls:

- 2 teaspoons (10 ml) sesame oil
- 1 shallot, minced
- 2 cloves garlic, minced
- 2 16oz. (945 ml) bags coleslaw mix
- 1 tablespoon (15 ml) soy sauce
- 1 tablespoon (15 ml) rice wine vinegar
- 1 teaspoon (5 ml) onion powder
- 1 teaspoon (5 ml) ground ginger
- 1 lb. (~20) egg roll wrappers
- 1 cup (235 ml) water
- 3 cups (710 ml) vegetable oil

Instructions

1. To make the plum sauce, combine the plum jam, apple cider vinegar, garlic powder, ground ginger, allspice, soy sauce, and water in a saucepan and set over medium-high heat.

2. Once the plum sauce comes to a boil, decrease the heat to medium-low heat and cook for 2 minutes, frequently stirring.
3. Allow the plum sauce to cool completely.
4. To make the egg rolls, place the sesame oil into the skillet and set over medium-high heat.
5. Add the shallots and garlic and cook for 2-3 minutes until the shallots are translucent.
6. Stir in the coleslaw mix, soy sauce, white wine vinegar, onion powder, and ginger and cook for 5-8 minutes, periodically stirring until the cabbage softens.
7. In batches, arrange the egg roll wrappers onto your workstation; leaving a 1-inch border, add 2-3 tablespoons of the coleslaw filling in the center of the wrappers.
8. Brush the edges of the egg roll wrappers with water, then fold one of the free edges of the dough over the filling.
9. Fold the other free edges of the filling over the dough, then dab the edges of the wrapper with water and fold them to seal the egg roll.
10. Place the egg rolls onto a parchment-lined cookie sheet, then add the vegetable oil to a deep skillet.
11. Once the oil comes to a temperature of 350°F (175°C), fry the egg rolls, seam side down in batches for 3-4 minutes per side until golden.
12. Drain the egg rolls on a wire rack, then arrange them on a serving platter with the plum sauce.
13. Serve and enjoy!

GLUTEN-FREE QUINOA MUSHROOM PATTIES

These quinoa mushroom patties are fried until golden, served on a bed of fresh peppery arugula leaves, and garnished tart yet sweet pomegranate seeds. Best of all, not only are these quinoa mushroom patties delicious, but they are also gluten-free.

Prep Time: 15 minutes| Cook Time: 35 minutes| Total Time: 50 minutes| Servings: 4

Ingredients

- 1 cup (235 ml) quinoa, rinsed
- 2 cups (470 ml) low-sodium vegetable broth
- ¼ cup (60 ml) ground flaxseed meal
- 6 tablespoons (90 ml) water
- 2 garlic cloves, minced
- 1 small shallot, minced
- 3 cups (710 ml) mushrooms, chopped
- 2 teaspoons (10 ml) olive oil
- 2 tablespoons (30 ml) freshly chopped parsley
- 1 teaspoon (5 ml) salt
- 1 teaspoon (5 ml) dried basil
- ¼ teaspoon (1 ml) black pepper
- ¼ teaspoon (1 ml) cayenne pepper
- 2 tablespoons (30 ml) tamari
- 2 tablespoons (30 ml) coconut aminos
- 1 ½ cups (255 ml) nutritional yeast
- ½ cup (120 ml) brown rice flour
- ¼ cup (60 ml) canola oil
- 2 cups (470 ml) arugula
- ½ cup (120 ml) pomegranate seeds

Instructions

1. Place the rinsed quinoa and vegetable broth into a pot and set it over medium-high heat.
2. Once the quinoa starts to boil, decrease the flame to medium-low and cook it covered for 15-20 minutes until the quinoa absorbs the vegetable broth.
3. Let the quinoa cool completely.
4. Whisk the flaxseed meal and water in a bowl and set aside for 5-10 minutes.

5. Place the olive oil into a frying pan and set it over medium-high heat.
6. Add the shallots and garlic and cook them for 1-2 minutes until translucent.
7. Add the mushrooms and cook them for 5-6 minutes until softened.
8. Transfer the mushroom mixture to a bowl along with the quinoa, parsley, salt, basil, black pepper, and cayenne pepper.
9. Add the flaxseed mixture, tamari, coconut aminos, nutritional yeast, and brown rice flour and mix to combine.
10. Divide the quinoa patties into 10 portions, form them into patties, then place them on a parchment-lined cookie sheet.
11. Place the canola oil into a non-stick skillet and set it over medium-high heat.
12. Add the quinoa patties, cook them for 3-4 minutes until golden, and then drain them on a paper towel-lined plate.
13. Arrange the arugula on a serving platter, then top with the quinoa patties and pomegranate seeds.
14. Serve and enjoy!

MUSHROOM WALNUT LEEK EMPANADAS

Filled with a hearty mushroom, leek, and walnut filling, these empanadas are baked until golden. These mushroom walnut leek empanadas are delicious and filling!

Prep Time: 35 minutes| Cook Time: 15 minutes|
Total Time: 50 minutes| Servings: 12

Ingredients

For the empanada dough:

- 3 cups (710 ml) all-purpose flour
- ½ cup (120 ml) cold vegan Earth Balance butter, cubed
- 1 teaspoon (5 ml) salt
- ½ - ¾ cups (120 ml – 180 ml) water

For the empanada filling:

- 2 tablespoons (30 ml) olive oil
- 1 bunch leeks, washed, dried, minced
- 2 cloves garlic, minced
- 1 lb. (~5 cups/~24 medium size) button mushrooms, minced
- 1 teaspoon (5 ml) smoked paprika
- 2 teaspoons (10 ml) dried thyme
- ½ teaspoon (2.5 ml) chili powder
- 1 teaspoon (5 ml) salt
- ¼ teaspoon (1 ml) black pepper
- 1 cup (235 ml) crushed walnuts

Instructions

1. Mix the all-purpose flour and salt in a bowl, then cut the cold vegan butter into the flour until the butter is the size of peas.
2. Beginning with ½ cup of water, add the water until a dough forms, adding more water in small portions if necessary.
3. Cover the empanada dough and let sit in the fridge for 15 minutes.
4. Place the olive oil into a skillet and set over medium-high heat.
5. Add the leeks and cook them for 3-5 minutes until they start to soften, then add the garlic and cook for 1 minute until fragrant.

6. Add the mushrooms, smoked paprika, dried thyme, chili powder, salt, and black pepper, and cook for 5-8 minutes until the mushrooms cook down.
7. Add the walnuts and cook for another 2 minutes, then remove the filling from the stove and let it cool slightly.
8. Turn your oven to 350°F (175°C), then line a cookie sheet with parchment paper.
9. Place the empanada dough onto a floured surface and divide it into 2 portions.
10. Roll each portion of the empanada dough until it is ¼-inch in size, then use a 4-inch circle cookie cutter to cut the dough into circles and place them onto the prepared cookie sheet.
11. Place 2 tablespoons of the filling onto one half of the dough, then dab the edges with water, pull the free edge of the dough over the filling, and use a fork to seal the dough.
12. Spray the empanadas with nonstick cooking spray and bake them for 15-20 minutes.
13. Serve and enjoy!

SIDE DISHES

- Spicy Sautéed Eggplant and Mushrooms
- Maple Balsamic Brussel Sprouts
- Curry Cauliflower Rice
- Christmas Wreath Salad
- Herb-roasted Carrots
- Swedish Carmelized Potatoes
- Indian Mushroom Rice Pilaf
- Green lentil Roasted Tomato Onion Salad
- Maple Roasted Root Vegetables
- Shaved Beet Chickpea Salad
- Dressing (Stuffing)
- Mashed Potatoes with Gravy

SPICY SAUTEED EGGPLANT AND MUSHROOMS

Fresh eggplants and mushrooms are sauteed to perfection along with shallots, garlic, and green chiles. With the perfect amount of spice, this is the perfect side dish to liven up your menu.

Prep Time: 10 minutes| Cook Time: 25 minutes|
Total Time: 35 minutes| Servings: 6-8

Ingredients

- 3 tablespoons (45 ml) olive oil
- 1 shallot, minced
- 1 green chili, seeds removed, minced
- 2 cloves garlic. minced
- 2 lb. (~8 cups/1890 ml) eggplant, peeled, chopped
- 1 lb. (~5 cups/~24 medium sized) mushrooms, chopped
- 1 teaspoon (5 ml) salt
- ¼ cup (60 ml) vegetable broth

Instructions

1. Place the olive oil into a non-stick skillet and set over medium-high heat.
2. Add the shallots and green chile and cook for 2-3 minutes, then add the garlic and cook it for 1 minute until fragrant.
3. Add the mushrooms and cook for 3-5 minutes until they start to soften.
4. Add the eggplant and salt, and cook them for 10 minutes until they start to soften.
5. Add the vegetable broth, decrease the flame to medium/low, and cook the eggplant and mushrooms covered for 5 minutes until the broth evaporates.
6. Serve and enjoy!

MAPLE BALSAMIC BRUSSELS SPROUTS

Brussel sprouts get jazzed up with a balsamic vinegar glaze that is salty yet sweet. They are the perfectly roasted side dish!

Prep Time: 10 minutes| Cook Time: 40 minutes| Total Time: 55 minutes| Servings: 4

Ingredients

- 1 lb. (~3 cups/~24 1-inch sized) Brussels sprouts, trimmed, halved
- 1 ½ tablespoons (22 ml) olive oil
- ½ teaspoon (2.5 ml) salt
- ¼ teaspoon (1 ml) black pepper
- 1 teaspoon (5 ml) garlic powder
- 2 tablespoons (30 ml) balsamic vinegar
- 2 tablespoons (30 ml) maple syrup

Instructions

1. Turn your oven to 400°F (205°C), then spray a baking dish with non-stick cooking spray.
2. Place the Brussel sprouts into a baking dish.
3. Whisk the olive oil, salt, pepper, garlic powder, balsamic vinegar, and maple syrup in a bowl, then add it to the Brussel sprouts and toss to combine.
4. Bake the maple syrup balsamic Brussel sprouts for 15-20 minutes, then turn them over and cook for an additional 15-20 minutes.
5. Serve and enjoy!

CURRY CAULIFLOWER RICE

This flavorful cauliflower rice is definitely not your plain old rice. Flavored with curry powder and paprika and topped with crunchy roasted pumpkin seeds, this low-carb cauliflower rice is simply amazing.

Prep Time: 3 minutes| Cook Time: 5 minutes| Total Time: 8 minutes| Servings: 4

Ingredients

- 2 tablespoons (30 ml) olive oil
- 1 small white onion, minced
- 2 cloves garlic, minced
- 1 teaspoon (5 ml) paprika
- 2 teaspoons (10 ml) curry powder
- 4 cups (945 ml) cauliflower rice
- 1 teaspoon (5 ml) salt
- ¼ cup (60 ml) roasted pumpkin seeds

Instructions

1. Add the olive oil into a skillet and set it over medium-high heat.
2. Add the onions and cook them for 2-3 minutes until they are translucent, then add the garlic, paprika, and curry powder and cook them for a minute until fragrant.
3. Stir in the cauliflower rice and cook for 4-5 minutes until the rice is heated through.
4. Stir in the pumpkin seeds and place the curry cauliflower rice into a serving dish.
5. Serve and enjoy!

CHRISTMAS WREATH SALAD

Not only is this Christmas wreath salad extremely delicious, but it is also beautiful. Layered with red carrots, beets, oranges, mangoes, and pomegranate seeds and dressed with a flavorful maple syrup mustard sauce, this salad is unlike anything you've ever had.

Prep Time: 20 minutes| Cook Time: 0 minutes| Total Time: 20 minutes| Servings: 6

Ingredients

For the salad:

- 8 oz. (1 cup/235 ml) salad greens
- 1 can sliced beets
- 1 mango, cut into slices
- 2 apples, sliced
- 1 red carrot, sliced into rounds
- 2 navel oranges, peeled, cut into half sections
- ½ cup (120 ml) pomegranate seeds

For the maple syrup mustard dressing:

- ¼ cup (60 ml) Dijon mustard
- ¼ cup (60 ml) extra-virgin olive oil
- ¼ cup (60 ml) apple cider vinegar
- 3 tablespoons (45 ml) maple syrup
- 2 garlic cloves, grated
- ¼ teaspoon (1 ml) sea salt
- ¼ teaspoon (1 ml) black pepper

Instructions

1. Arrange the salad greens onto 6 serving dishes and set aside.
2. Use star-shaped cookie cutters to cut star shaped beet and mango slices.
3. Place the beets onto the salad greens, then top with the apples, carrots, orange sections, pomegranate seeds, and mangoes.
4. For the maple syrup mustard salad dressing, whisk the Dijon mustard, olive oil, apple cider vinegar, maple syrup, garlic, sea salt, and pepper.
5. Pour the maple syrup mustard dressing over the Christmas wreath salad.
6. Serve and enjoy!

HERB ROASTED CARROTS

Fresh carrots are coated in a savory yet sweet seasoning mix that includes garlic, maple syrup, thyme rosemary, and basil. These flavorful herb-roasted carrots will add flavor to any meal!

Prep Time: 5 minutesl Cook Time: 35 minutesl
Total Time: 40 minutesl Servings: 4

Ingredients

- 2 tablespoons (30 ml) olive oil
- 1 teaspoon (5 ml) garlic powder
- 1 teaspoon (5 ml) thyme
- 1 teaspoon (5 ml) rosemary
- ½ teaspoon (2.5 ml) basil
- ½ teaspoon (2.5 ml) dried parsley
- ½ teaspoon (2.5 ml) salt
- 1 teaspoon (5 ml) maple syrup
- ¼ teaspoon (1 ml) black pepper
- 1 lb. (~2½ cups/590 ml) carrots, peeled, cut into ½-inch rounds

Instructions

1. Turn your oven to 375°F (190°C), then lightly grease a cast iron skillet with cooking spray.
2. Whisk the olive oil, garlic powder, Italian seasoning, parsley, salt, maple syrup, and pepper in a bowl.
3. Add the carrots and toss to combine.
4. Place the carrots into the prepared cast-iron skillet in an even layer and bake them for 35 minutes until tender.
5. Serve and enjoy!

SWEDISH CARAMELIZED POTATOES

No Christmas day meal is complete without a side of potatoes. This twist on a Swedish classic Christmas dish features baby potatoes coated in a sweet caramel sauce with a touch of cayenne pepper for added spice and flavor.

Prep Time: 15 minutes| Cook Time: 35 minutes|
Total Time: 50 minutes| Servings: 6

Ingredients

- 2 ¼ pounds (~7 cups/1650 ml) baby potatoes, rinsed
- 2 tablespoons (30 ml) salt
- ½ cup (120 ml) granulated sugar
- 2 tablespoons (30 ml) vegan Earth Balance butter
- ½ teaspoon (2.5 ml) cayenne pepper

Instructions

1. Place the baby potatoes and salt into a pot and cover with water.
2. Place the baby potatoes over medium-high heat and cook for 15 minutes until fork tender.
3. Drain the potatoes, let cool slightly, then peel them and chill for 15-20 minutes.
4. Sprinkle the granulated sugar onto the bottom of a skillet, set it over medium-low heat, and cook until it melts and darkens around the edges. Do not stir the sugar.
5. Add the butter, stir until it becomes a syrup, then stir in the cayenne pepper.
6. Place the baby potatoes into a colander, lightly rinse them with cold water and drain them.
7. Add the potatoes to the caramel, toss them around and cool them for 6-8 minutes until they are warmed through.
8. Serve and enjoy!

INDIAN MUSHROOM RICE PILAF

This Indian mushroom pilaf is irresistibly delicious. Flavored by spices such as cardamom, cloves, cumin, and fennel, studded with mushrooms and cashews, and topped with fried spinach, you've never had rice pilaf this way.

Prep Time: 30 minutes| Cook Time: 23 minutes|
Total Time: 53 minutes| Servings: 4

Ingredients

For the rice pilaf:

- 1 cup (235 ml) basmati rice
- 1 ½ cups (355 ml) water
- 3 tablespoons (45 ml) Earth Balance vegan butter
- ¼ teaspoon (1 ml) fennel seeds
- ¼ teaspoon (1 ml) cumin seeds
- 2 whole cloves
- 1 teaspoon (5 ml) ground cardamom
- 2 shallots, sliced thinly
- 2 cloves garlic, minced
- 1 cup (235 ml) cashews
- 8 oz. (1 cup/235 ml) mushrooms, sliced
- 2 finger chilis, minced
- 2 bay leaves
- 1 teaspoon (5 ml) salt
- 1 teaspoon (5 ml) dried basil
- 2 cups (470 ml) vegetable broth

For the fried spinach:

- 1 cup (235 ml) vegetable oil
- 1 cup (235 ml) spinach, washed, dried, roughly chopped

For the salad:

- juice of 1 lime
- 3 tablespoons (45 ml) olive oil
- 1 teaspoon (5 ml) salt
- ½ teaspoon (2.5ml) black pepper
- 1 large tomato, diced
- 1 red onion, diced

Instructions

1. Place the basmati rice into a pot, cover with water and soak for 30 minutes.
2. Place the butter into a pot and set it over medium-high heat.
3. Add the fennel seeds, cumin seeds, cloves, and cardamom and cook for 1 minute until fragrant.
4. Stir in the shallots and minced garlic and cook for 1-2 minutes until the shallots are translucent.
5. Stir in the cashew and cook for an additional 1-2 minutes until lightly golden.
6. Stir in the mushrooms and finger chilis, salt, bay leaves, and dried basil and cook for 4-5 minutes until the mushrooms soften.
7. Drain the soaked basmati rice and rice 5-6 times until the water runs clear and most of the starch is removed.
8. Add the basmati rice to the mushroom mixture and cook for 1 minute, stirring frequently, then add the vegetable broth to the pot, cover it with the lid and allow it to cook for 10-11 minutes.
9. Turn the flame off and allow the Indian mushroom rice pilaf to sit covered for 4-5 minutes.
10. Fluff the Indian mushroom rice pilaf with a fork.
11. To make the fried spinach, place the vegetable oil in a pot, set over medium-high heat.
12. Once the oil comes to a temperature of 350°F (175°C), add the spinach and cook for 2-3 minutes until crispy, then drain it on a paper towel-lined plate.
13. To make the salad, whisk the lime juice, olive oil, salt, and pepper in a bowl, then add the tomatoes and onions and toss to combine.
14. Place the Indian mushroom pilaf into a serving bowl, top it with the fried spinach and serve with the tomato onion salad.
15. Serve and enjoy!

GREEN LENTIL ONION TOMATO SALAD

This green lentil salad is bursting with flavor. Fresh tomatoes and onions are roasted to perfection then added to a green lentil salad drenched in a sweet yet citrus-flavored grapefruit basil dressing.

Prep Time: 15 minutes| Cook Time: 50 minutes|
Total Time: 1 hour 5 minutes| Servings: 4

Ingredients

For the roasted tomatoes and onions:

- ½ lb. (~¾ cup/180 ml or ~10) cherry tomatoes, halved
- 1 cup (235 ml) onion, sliced
- 4 tablespoons (60 ml) olive oil
- ½ teaspoon (2.5 ml) salt
- 1 teaspoon (5 ml) basil
- ½ teaspoon (2.5 ml) black pepper

For the lentil salad:

- 1 ½ cup (355 ml) green lentils, rinsed
- ½ teaspoon (2.5 ml) salt
- 2 cloves garlic, minced
- 1 celery stalk, diced

For the grapefruit basil dressing:

- juice of 1 grapefruit
- ¼ cup (60 ml) olive oil
- 1 teaspoon (5 ml) dried basil
- 1 teaspoon (5 ml) onion powder
- ½ teaspoon (2.5 ml) cayenne pepper
- ½ teaspoon (2.5 ml) salt

Instructions

1. Heat your oven to 425°F (220°C).
2. Place the cherry tomatoes, onion, olive oil, salt, basil, and pepper in a baking dish and toss to combine.

3. Spread the cherry tomatoes into an even layer, then roast the tomatoes for 15-20 minutes until the skins start to burst, then allow them to cool completely.
4. To make the lentils, place them into a saucepan along with the salt, and add enough water to cover the lentils.
5. Cover the lentils and allow them to cook for 20-30 minutes until they are tender, then drain the cooked lentils and let them cool completely.
6. Combine the lentils, garlic, and celery in a large bowl.
7. To make the grapefruit basil dressing, combine the grapefruit juice, olive oil, basil, cayenne pepper, and salt in a bowl, then pour the dressing over the lentil mixture.
8. Place the lentil salad into a serving dish and top with the roasted tomatoes and onions.
9. Serve and enjoy!

MAPLE ROASTED ROOT VEGETABLES

Carrots, parsnips, rutabagas, and shallots are coated with a glaze consisting of fresh savory garlic and rosemary, sweet maple syrup, olive oil, and balsamic vinegar and roasted to perfection.

Prep Time: 10 minutes| Cook Time: 45 minutes|
Total Time: 55 minutes| Servings: 6

Ingredients

- 3 cloves garlic, minced
- 1 tablespoon (15 ml) fresh rosemary
- 4 tablespoons (60 ml) olive oil
- 2 tablespoons (30 ml) maple syrup
- 1 tablespoon (15 ml) balsamic vinegar
- 1 teaspoon (5 ml) sea salt
- 3 large shallots, sliced into quarters
- 2 large turnips, peeled diced into large cubes
- 15 parsnips, peeled
- 15 carrots, peeled

Instructions

1. Heat your oven to 400°F (205°C).
2. Whisk the garlic, rosemary, olive oil, maple syrup, balsamic vinegar, and salt in a bowl.
3. Place the shallots, turnips, parsnips, and carrots onto a cookie sheet lined with parchment paper, then add the garlic maple syrup mixture and toss to combine.
4. Spread the vegetable mixture into an even layer and cook for 22 minutes.
5. Turn the vegetables over and cook for an additional 10-12 minutes until they are tender and golden.
6. Serve and enjoy!

SHAVED BEET CHICKPEA SALAD

Wow your friends and family at Christmas with this shaved beet chickpea salad. Featuring roasted beast, chickpeas, lamb's lettuce and a balsamic lemon dressing that is absolutely delicious.

Prep Time: 10 minutes| Cook Time: 55 minutes|
Total Time: 1 hour 5 minutes| Servings: 6

Ingredients

- 2 lbs. (6-8 medium sized) fresh, beets, scrubbed, thoroughly washed
- 1 teaspoon (5 ml) salt
- ½ teaspoon (2.5 ml) black pepper
- 4 tablespoons (60 ml) olive oil
- 4 cups (945 ml) lambs lettuce (also known as corn salad)
- 1 15 oz. (445 ml) can chickpeas
- juice of one lemon
- 2 tablespoons (30 ml) balsamic vinegar
- 3 tablespoons (45 ml) fresh thyme, chopped

Instructions

1. Turn your oven to 450°F (220°C).
2. Remove the beets tops and bottoms, place them into a baking dish and massage them with salt, black pepper, and 1 tablespoon olive oil.
3. Cover the beets tightly with aluminum foil and bake them for 45-55 minutes until tender.
4. Allow the beets to cool completely.
5. Arrange the lamb's lettuce onto serving dishes or a serving platter.
6. Shave the beets into thin slices or slice them thinly, then add them to the lettuce and top it with the chickpeas.
7. Whisk the remaining olive oil, lemon juice, balsamic vinegar, and thyme in a bowl, then place it into a serving dish.
8. Serve and enjoy!

DRESSING (STUFFING)

You won't believe the flavors in this made from scratch dressing! Made in a pan, this is the secret dish to making your meal classic!

Prep Time: 1 hour, 15 minutes!
Cook Time: 35 minutes!
Total Time: 1 hour and 50 minutes! Servings: 8

Ingredients

- 1 – 2 tablespoons (15-30 ml) olive oil
- 4 stalks of celery, chopped
- ½ medium onion chopped
- 6 slices whole grain bread, or your bread of choice, torn into 1-2 inch pieces and allowed to air dry 1-2 hours.
- 1 teaspoon (5 ml) poultry seasonings
- 1 teaspoon (5 ml) Herbamare seasoning or other seasoning saltines
- Your choice of fresh herbs - sprigs of parsley, rosemary, sage and/or thyme. Stems removed and chopped finely.
- Sea salt to taste
- ⅛ teaspoon (.6 ml) pepper
- up to ¾ cup (180 ml) water or vegetable broth

Instructions

1. In a large frying pan, sauté celery and onion in the olive oil until softened. Add bread pieces and stir to mix well.
2. While mixture is cooking, for up to 10 minutes on low, add poultry seasoning, Herbamare and fresh herbs.
3. Drizzle mixture with water or vegetable broth and stir frequently. Add the liquid in ¼ cup increments untill desired moistness is achieved,
4. Adjust seasoning to taste with salt and poultry seasoning.
5. Pack mixture into a medium casserole dish. Use the back of a large spoon to press it down.

6. Bake at 325°F (160°C) in the oven for 20 minutes to blend the flavors.
7. Serve with cranberry sauce and enjoy!

MASHED POTATOES AND GRAVY

These amazing mashed potatoes and vegan gravy will fool everyone. Nobody will believe it's 100% vegan!

Prep Time: 40 minutes| Cook Time: 40 minutes|
Total Time: 1 hour and 20 minutes| Servings: 8

Ingredients

For the potatoes:

- 8 large white potatoes
- 2 tablespoons (30 ml) Earth Balance butter
- ¼ cup (60 ml) soy, almond or rice milk
- ½ teaspoon (2.5 ml) salt
- 2 tablespoons (30 ml) finely diced onions (optional)

For the Gravy:

- 2 tablespoons (30 ml) olive oil
- 1 cup (235 ml) chopped onion
- 1 clove garlic
- ½ cup (120 ml) whole wheat flour
- 3 cups + 1 cup (4 cups total/945 ml) vegetable broth
- 1 teaspoon (5 ml) poultry seasoning
- 2 tablespoons (30 ml) tamari or shoyu sauce
- 3 tablespoons (45 ml) nutritional yeast
- 2 tablespoons (30 ml) miso paste
- 1 teaspoon (5 ml) onion powder
- salt and pepper to taste

Instructions

For the potatoes:

1. Peel and cut the potatoes into quarters.
2. Boil for 20 minutes until soft, do not overcook.
3. Drain potatoes, rinse and mash with a potato masher

4. Add in butter, milk, salt and onions, mix thoroughly.
5. Cover with tin foil and keep warm in the oven while you make the gravy.

For the gravy:

1. Heat the olive oil in a large frying pan.
2. Add onion and garlic. Cook until well-done stirring frequently. Add in 3 cups of vegetable broth, continue to heat and stir together.
3. Place the reserved cup of vegetable broth in a glass jar and add ½ cup whole wheat flour. Shake until flour is completely dissolved. Be sure to add the broth to the jar first to avoid clumping.
4. Add the flour/broth mixture to the pan and stir constantly until thick.
5. Continue to cook and add in 2 tablespoons tamari or shoyu sauce, poultry seasoning, nutritional yeast, miso paste, onion powder, salt and pepper.
6. When gravy has thickened, allow to cool slightly to avoid hot splashes and purée with a stick blender or place in a regular blender until silky smooth.
7. Reheat and adjust the seasoning if needed.
8. Serve with mashed potatoes and enjoy!

MAIN DISHES

- Quinoa Lentil Nut Meatloaf
- Veggie Pot Pie
- Roasted Cauliflower Steaks
- Shepard's Pie
- Spinach Basil Trottole with Pesto Sauce
- Roasted Cabbage Steaks
- Spiced Chickpea Stuffed Sweet Potatoes
- Warm Green Pea Brocolli Pasta
- Indian Lentil Daal Curry
- Mushroom Stuffed Cabbage Rolls
- Tomato Bean Carrot Stew
- Peanut Spinach Pesto Gnocchi
- White Spinach Mushroom Pinenut Lasagna
- Potato Pear Casserole
- Butternut Squash Cranberry Wellington

QUINOA LENTIL NUT MEATLOAF

Featuring lentils, quinoa, mushrooms, carrots, walnuts, onion, garlic, and so much more, this quinoa lentil nut meatloaf is irresistibly delicious. Coated with a sweet yet zesty glaze, this meatloaf cooks in 40 minutes.

Prep Time: 30 minutes| Cook Time: 45 minutes|
Chill Time: 5 minutes|
Total Time: 1 hour, 20 minutes| Servings: 10

Ingredients

For the meatloaf:

- 2 tablespoons (30 ml) olive oil
- 1 small onion, diced
- 1 small yellow bell pepper, diced
- 1 cup (235 ml) diced carrots
- 1 cup (235 ml) chopped mushrooms
- 2 garlic cloves minced
- 1 teaspoon (5 ml) salt
- ½ teaspoon (2.5 ml) black pepper
- 1 ½ cups (355 ml) cooked lentils
- ⅔ cup (160 ml) breadcrumbs
- ½ cup (120 ml) pecans
- ½ cup (120 ml) cooked quinoa
- ½ cup (120 ml) rolled oats
- 3 tablespoons (45 ml) vegan parmesan cheese
- 1 tablespoon (15 ml) ground flaxseed meal
- ½ cup (120 ml) tomato paste
- 2 tablespoons (30 ml) coconut aminos
- 1 tablespoon (15 ml) maple syrup
- 2 teaspoons (10 ml) Italian seasoning

For the glaze:

- 2 tablespoons (30 ml) tomato paste
- 2 teaspoons (10 ml) lemon juice
- 2 teaspoons (10 ml) granulated sugar
- ½ teaspoon (2.5 ml) mustard powder
- ½ teaspoon (2.5 ml) coconut aminos

Instructions

1. Turn your oven to 350°F (175°C), then line a 9x5-inch loaf pan with parchment and set it aside.
2. Place the olive oil into a non-stick skillet and set it over medium-high heat.
3. Add the onions and bell peppers and cook them for 3 minutes.
4. Stir in the carrots, mushrooms, and garlic and cook it for 5-7 minutes until softened, then stir in the salt and pepper.
5. Transfer the mushroom carrot mixture to a food processor's bowl along with 1 cup of cooked lentils, breadcrumbs, pecans, quinoa, oats, vegan parmesan cheese, flaxseed, tomato paste, coconut aminos, maple syrup, and Italian seasoning and blend until a dough begins to form.
6. Add the remaining ½ cup of lentils and pulse to combine.
7. Place the meatloaf batter into the prepared pan, smoothing it into an even layer with a spatula.
8. To make the glaze, whisk the tomato paste, lemon juice, granulated sugar, mustard powder, and coconut aminos in a bowl and brush it over the meatloaf.
9. Bake the quinoa lentil nut meatloaf for 45 minutes, then let it cool for 5 minutes before slicing.
10. Serve and enjoy!

VEGGIE POT PIE

This pot pie features mushrooms and potatoes and is flavored by shallots, celery, carrots, garlic, and fresh thyme. Baked until golden, these pot pies are a delicious serving of comfort.

Prep Time: 25 minutes| Cook Time: 25 minutes|
Total Time: 50 minutes| Servings: 6

Ingredients

- 2 tablespoons (30 ml) olive oil
- 2 tablespoons (30 ml) vegan Earth Balance butter
- 2 medium shallots, chopped
- 4 cloves garlic, minced
- 2 stalks celery, diced
- 8 oz. (1 cup/235 ml) button mushrooms diced
- 2 large carrots, diced
- 4 large potatoes, diced
- 3 sprigs fresh thyme. removed from the stem
- 1 teaspoon (5 ml) salt
- ½ teaspoon (2.5 ml) black pepper
- ¼ teaspoon (1 ml) paprika
- ½ cup (120 ml) white wine
- ¼ cup (60 ml) all-purpose flour
- 1 ¼ cups (295 ml) vegetable stock
- ¼ cup + 2 tablespoons (90 ml) coconut milk
- 1 large sheet of vegan puff pastry

Instructions

1. Turn your oven to 400°F (205°C), and spray a large round baking dish with non-stick cooking spray.
2. Place the olive oil and butter into a pot, add the shallots, garlic, and celery to the pot, and cook it for 4-5 minutes until the onions are translucent.
3. Add the carrots and mushrooms and cook for an additional 5 minutes until the mushrooms are softened.

4. Stir in the potatoes, thyme, salt, pepper, and paprika, and cook for an additional 5-8 minutes until the mushrooms and potatoes start to turn brown.
5. Stir in the white wine, scraping your spoon against the bottom of the pot to release the bits of flavor, and cook for 4-5 minutes until the wine evaporates.
6. Stir in the all-purpose flour until a paste forms, then gradually add the stock, constantly stirring until the sauce is thick and creamy.
7. Next, add ¼ cup of coconut milk, stir to combine then transfer the vegetable pot pie into the prepared baking dish and place the puff pastry on top, making sure to tuck the edges under to create a crust.
8. Shape the edges of the crust into a fluted shape, so it does not hang over the sides of the dish and poke the puff pastry with a fork to keep it from exploding in the oven.
9. Brush the veggie pot pie with the remaining 2 tablespoons of coconut milk and bake for 25-30 minutes until golden.
10. Let the veggie pot pie sit for 5 minutes.
11. Serve and enjoy!

ROASTED CAULIFLOWER STEAKS

These cauliflower steaks are light, delicious, and perfect for Christmas dinner. Featuring spices such as smoked paprika, cumin, turmeric, and nutritional yeast, these steaks are golden and delicious.

Prep Time: 10 minutes| Cook Time: 20 minutes| Total Time: 30 minutes| Servings: 4

Ingredients

- 1 medium cauliflower head, leaves, stem removed
- 3 tablespoons (45 ml) olive oil
- ¼ cup (60 ml) nutritional yeast
- 1 teaspoon (5 ml) smoked paprika
- ⅛ teaspoon (.6 ml) turmeric
- ¼ teaspoon (1 ml) cumin
- 1 teaspoon (5 ml) garlic powder
- 1 teaspoon (5 ml) onion powder
- ½ teaspoon (2.5 ml) dried basil
- 1 teaspoon (5 ml) salt
- ¼ teaspoon (1 ml) cayenne pepper
- ¼ teaspoon (1 ml) black pepper
- 2 tablespoons (30 ml) freshly chopped parsley

Instructions

1. Turn your oven to 400°F (205°C), then grease a large cast-iron skillet with non-stick spray.
2. Cut the head of cauliflower into 1-inch steaks, then place them into a baking dish.
3. Whisk the olive oil, nutritional yeast, smoked paprika, turmeric, cumin, garlic powder, onion powder, basil, salt, cayenne, and pepper in a bowl.
4. Add the seasoning olive oil mixture to the cauliflower and gently massage the seasoning into the cauliflower.
5. Place the cauliflower into the prepared cast-iron skillet and bake for 20 minutes until tender, then garnish with the chopped parsley.
6. Serve and enjoy!

SHEPHERD'S PIE

This Shepard's pie has a creamy, crispy layer of mashed potatoes that hides a hearty savory filling made from parsnips, carrots, green peas, and mushrooms. With a smooth, delicious white wine gravy, this Shepard's pie is utterly amazing.

Prep Time: 30 minutes| Cook Time: 25 minutes|
Total Time: 55 minutes| Servings: 4

Ingredients

For the mashed potatoes:

- 2 lb. (~5 cups/1180 ml) medium potatoes, peeled, diced
- 2 garlic cloves
- 1 ½ teaspoons (7.5 ml) salt
- ¼ cup (60 ml) vegan Earth Balance butter
- ½ cup (120 ml) coconut milk
- ¼ cup (60 ml) vegan parmesan cheese

For the filling:

- 2 tablespoons (30 ml) olive oil
- 1 large red onion, diced
- 1 green pepper, diced
- 4 cloves garlic, minced
- 1 tablespoon (15 ml) fresh thyme
- 1 medium carrot, diced
- 1 medium parsnip, diced
- 1 lb. (~6 cups/1415 ml) button mushrooms, sliced
- 2 bay leaves
- ½ teaspoon (2.5 ml) white pepper
- 1 tablespoon (15 ml) smoked paprika
- 1 teaspoon (5 ml) salt
- ½ teaspoon (2.5 ml) black pepper
- 1 teaspoon (5 ml) dried basil
- 3 tablespoons (45 ml) all-purpose flour
- 2 cups (470 ml) low-sodium vegetable broth
- ½ cup (120 ml) white wine
- 1 cup (235 ml) frozen green peas

Instructions

1. Place the diced potatoes, garlic, and salt into a pot and cover them with water.
2. Cook the potatoes over medium-high heat for 12-15 minutes until tender, then drain them and remove the garlic cloves.
3. Next, place the cooked potatoes back into the pot and add the vegan butter, coconut milk, parmesan cheese, and pepper and mash the potatoes until they are creamy.
4. Turn your oven to 350°F (175°).
5. To make the Shepard's pie filling, place the olive oil into a pot and set it over medium-high heat.
6. Add the diced red onion and green bell pepper and cook for 5 minutes until the onions are translucent.
7. Stir in the minced garlic and fresh thyme and cook for 1-2 minutes until fragrant.
8. Stir in the carrots, parsnips, and mushrooms and cook for 5-10 minutes until they start to soften.
9. Add the bay leaves, paprika, salt, pepper, and dried basil, cook for 30 seconds, then add the all-purpose flour and cook for 1-2 minutes.
10. Stir in the white wine and vegetable broth, whisking until the sauce is smooth, and cook for 10 minutes.
11. Next, add the frozen green peas and cook for 2-3 minutes.
12. Transfer the Shepard's pie filling to an 8 x 9 baking dish and spread into an even layer.
13. Place the mashed potatoes on top of the filling and spread into an even layer.
14. With a fork, create indentations in the mashed potatoes, then bake for 25 minutes.
15. Serve and enjoy!

SPINACH BASIL TROTTOLE WITH PESTO SAUCE

This simple pasta dish is so delicious it will knock your socks off. Trottle pasta, fresh basil leaves, spinach, and capers are coated with a freshly made pesto to create a main dish that is so elegant it will wow your dinner guests.

Prep Time: 15 minutes| Cook Time: 15 minutes|
Total Time: 30 minutes| Servings:4

Ingredients

For the pesto:

- ½ cup (120 ml) pine nuts
- 2 cups (470 ml) fresh basil
- ⅓ cup (80 ml) nutritional yeast
- ⅓ cup (80 ml) olive oil
- 1 teaspoon (5 ml) salt
- ½ teaspoon (2.5 ml) black pepper
- 2 tablespoons (30 ml) lemon juice
- 3 cloves garlic minced
- 1 small shallot, minced

For the pasta:

- 1 17-ounce (500 ml) package tri-colored trottole pasta
- 1 cup (235 ml) fresh spinach
- ½ cup (120 ml) fresh basil leaves
- 1-1¼ cup (235-295 ml) pesto
- ⅓ cup (80 ml) capers
- 3 tablespoons (45 ml) nutritional yeast

Instructions

1. To make the pesto, place the pine nuts into a skillet and toast for 5-8 minutes until brown.
2. Take the toasted pine nuts out of the skillet and set them aside to cool slightly.
3. Add the pine nuts, basil, nutritional yeast, and olive oil to a food processor's bowl and blend until it reaches your desired consistency.
4. Add the salt, pepper, lemon juice, garlic, and shallots and blend a few times until combined.

5. To prepare the pasta, boil the trottle according to the manufacturer's instructions, then drain them and rinse them with cold water.
6. Place the trottle pasta into a serving dish and add the spinach, basil, pesto, capers, and nutritional yeast and toss to combine.
7. Serve and enjoy!

ROASTED CABBAGE STEAKS

These roasted cabbage steaks are a dream come true. They are golden, beautiful, slightly charred, tender on the inside, and coated with smoked paprika, garlic powder, and nutritional yeast for an extra dose of flavor!

Prep Time: 10 minutes| Cook Time: 25 minutes| Total Time: 35 minutes| Servings: 4

Ingredients

- 2 small heads of cabbage
- 3 tablespoons (45 ml) olive oil
- 1 teaspoon (5 ml) salt
- ½ teaspoon (2.5 ml) black pepper
- 2 teaspoons (10 ml) paprika
- 1 teaspoon (5 ml) garlic powder
- 1 teaspoon (5 ml) onion powder
- 2 tablespoons (30 ml) nutritional yeast

Instructions

1. Turn your oven to 400°F (205°C), then line a cookie sheet with parchment paper.
2. Slice the stems off the cabbages, then slice each cabbage in half and cut each half into 1-inch steaks.
3. Arrange the 4 cabbage steaks onto the prepared cookie sheet leaving a few inches of space between each steak.
4. Brush each cabbage steak with olive oil, then whisk the salt, pepper, garlic powder, smoked paprika, and nutritional yeast in a small bowl.
5. Gently massage half of the seasoning into the cabbage steaks, then turn them over and repeat the process.
6. Bake the cabbage steaks for 15 minutes until it is golden and tender.
7. Serve and enjoy!

SPICED CHICKPEA STUFFED SWEET POTATOES

Sweet potatoes are roasted to perfection, then topped with crispy, tender spiced roasted chickpeas and tahini. It is a filling and hearty meal that's guaranteed to earn you a round of applause.

Prep Time: 10 minutes| Cook Time: 1 hour|
Total Time: 1 hour 10 minutes| Serves: 4

Ingredients

- 4 medium sweet potatoes
- 1 15 oz. (445 ml) can chickpeas, drained, rinsed
- 1 tablespoon (15 ml) olive oil
- 1 teaspoon (5 ml) salt
- ½ teaspoon (2.5 ml) cumin
- 2 teaspoons (10 ml) smoked paprika
- ½ teaspoon (2.5 ml) cayenne pepper
- 1 clove garlic, minced
- 2 tablespoons (30 ml) tahini
- 2 tablespoons (30 ml) freshly chopped parsley

Instructions

1. Turn your oven to 375°F (190°C), poke the sweet potatoes with a fork, then place them onto a cookie sheet and roast them for 45-55 minutes until tender.
2. At the same time, place the chickpeas into a bowl, add the olive oil, salt, cumin, smoked paprika, cayenne pepper, and garlic powder, and toss to combine.
3. Place the chickpeas onto a parchment-lined cookie sheet and bake them for 25-35 minutes until crispy, turning them at the 15-minute mark.
4. Let the roasted sweet potatoes cool for 5-10 minutes, then cut them in half lengthwise and remove the sweet potatoes flesh, mash flesh with Earth Balance butter and salt.
5. Fill each potato shell with the mixture, add the chickpeas on top and top with the tahini and parsley.
6. Serve and enjoy!

WARM GREEN PEA BROCCOLI PASTA

Warm pasta shells, broccoli florets, and green peas are combined with a flavorful broccoli sauce. This hearty warm green pea broccoli pasta is delicious and flavorful!

Prep Time: 5 minutes| Cook Time: 15 minutes|
Total Time: 20 minutes| Servings: 4

Ingredients

- 1 ½ heads broccoli, stem removed, cut into florets
- 4 cloves garlic, peeled
- 1 small shallot, diced
- ½ cup (120 ml) cashew milk
- ½ teaspoon (2.5 ml) black pepper
- ½ teaspoon (2.5 ml) salt
- 2 tablespoons (30 ml) nutritional yeast
- 1 lb. (~4¾ cups/1115 ml) pasta shells
- 1 cup (235 ml) frozen green peas

Instructions

1. Place the broccoli florets into a pot of water and cook them for 3-4 minutes until tender.
2. Reserve 1 cup of broccoli florets and place the remaining florets into the blender along with the garlic, shallots, cashew milk, pepper, salt, and nutritional yeast in a blender and blend into a smooth sauce.
3. Prepare the pasta shells according to the manufacturer's instructions and add the green peas during the final 2-3 minutes of cooking time.
4. Drain the pasta and green peas, add them to a bowl along with the reserved broccoli and broccoli sauce and toss to combine.
5. Serve and enjoy!

INDIAN LENTIL DAAL CURRY

Filled with tender potatoes, carrots, and lentils, this Indian lentil Daal curry is hearty and delicious. Serve with the Indian mushroom rice pilaf or curry cauliflower rice for best results.

Prep Time: 10 minutes| Cook Time: 25 minutes|
Total Time: 35 minutes| Servings: 8

Ingredients

- 2 tablespoons (30 ml) olive oil
- 2 medium onions, finely diced
- 1 celery stalk, diced
- 1 yellow bell pepper, minced
- 1 tablespoon (30 ml) fresh ginger, grated
- 2 cloves garlic, minced
- 1 tablespoon (15 ml) mild red curry paste
- 2 teaspoons (10 ml) ground turmeric
- 2 teaspoons (10 ml) tomato paste
- 1 teaspoon (5 ml) salt
- ½ teaspoon (2.5 ml) black pepper
- 3 large carrots, peeled and diced
- 3 potatoes, peeled, diced
- 1 ½ cup (355 ml) split green lentils
- 5 cups (1190 ml) vegetable broth
- 1 cup (235 ml) full fat coconut milk
- 2 tablespoons (30 ml) freshly chopped cilantro

Instructions

1. Add the olive oil into a pot and set it over medium-high heat.
2. Add the onions, bell peppers, ginger, and garlic and cook for 3-5 minutes until the onions are translucent.
3. Stir in the curry paste, turmeric, tomato paste, salt, and pepper and cook for 1 minute until fragrant.
4. Stir in the carrots, potatoes, and lentils, then add the vegetable broth.
5. Cover the Indian Daal curry and allow it to come to a boil, and cook for 25-30 minutes until the lentils and potatoes are tender.

6. Decrease the flame to medium-low, stir in the coconut milk and cilantro, and allow it to cook for 2 minutes.
7. Serve and enjoy!

MUSHROOM STUFFED CABBAGE ROLLS

Cabbage leaves are stuffed with rice, mushrooms, and herbs, then baked in fresh tomato sauce until tender. These mushroom cabbage rolls are delicious and filling!

Prep Time: 25 minutes
Cook Time: 1 hour 15 minutes
Total Time: 1 hour 40 minutes Servings: 5

Ingredients

For the tomato sauce:

- 2 tablespoons (30 ml) olive oil
- 2 medium shallots, diced
- 3 cloves garlic, minced
- 2 tablespoons (30 ml) tomato paste
- 1 28 oz. (830 ml) can crushed tomatoes
- 2 tablespoons (30 ml) apple cider vinegar
- 1 tablespoon (15 ml) maple syrup
- 2 teaspoons (10 ml) dried basil
- ½ teaspoon (2.5 ml) salt
- ¼ teaspoon (1 ml) black pepper

For the cabbage rolls:

- 15 cabbage leaves
- 2 tablespoons (30 ml) olive oil
- 1 small onion, diced
- ½ red bell pepper, diced
- 1 lb. (~6 cups/1430 ml) button mushrooms, diced
- 1 ½ cups (355 ml) uncooked white rice
- ½ cup (120 ml) Italian breadcrumbs
- 2 tablespoons (30 ml) freshly chopped parsley
- ½ teaspoon (2.5 ml) salt
- ¼ teaspoon (1 ml) black pepper

Instructions

1. To make the tomato sauce, place the olive oil into a saucepot and set it over medium-high heat.
2. Add the chopped shallots and cook for 2-3 minutes until translucent, then add the garlic and cook for 1 minute until fragrant.

3. Stir in the tomato paste, maple syrup, and apple cider vinegar and cook for another minute.
4. Add the crushed tomatoes and basil and decrease the heat to medium-low and allow the tomato sauce to cook for 20 minutes.
5. To make the stuffed cabbage, blanch the cabbage leaves in a large pot of boiling water for 1 minute until tender and pliable, then drain them and set them aside.
6. Turn your oven to 350°F (175°C), then place the olive oil into a deep skillet and set it over medium-high heat.
7. Add the chopped onions and red bell peppers and cook for 3-5 minutes until softened.
8. Stir in the button mushrooms and cook them for 4-5 minutes until softened.
9. Add the rice, one cup of tomato sauce, bread crumbs, parsley, salt, and pepper, stir to combine, and remove it from the heat.
10. To assemble the cabbage rolls, remove the tough white vein running through the center of the cabbage leaves, then add ⅓ cup of filling on one end of the cabbage.
11. Roll the cabbage leaves up, making sure to tuck the sides as you roll it.
12. Place remaining tomato sauce into the bottom of a 9 by 13-inch dish and arrange the cabbage rolls seam side down into the dish.
13. Cover the cabbage rolls with aluminum foil and bake for 1 hour and 15 minutes.
14. Serve and enjoy!

TOMATO BEAN CARROT STEW

This comforting protein-rich stew is loaded with flavor. Studded with beans, carrots, and tomatoes, this bean tomato carrot stew is filled with delicious, rich tomato flavor.

Prep Time: 5 minutes| Cook Time: 20 minutes|
Total Time: 20 minutes| Servings: 3

Ingredients

- 2 tablespoons (30 ml) olive oil
- 1 red onion, diced
- 2 cloves garlic, minced
- 1 teaspoon (5 ml) salt
- ½ teaspoon (2.5 ml) black pepper
- 1 teaspoon (5 ml) smoked paprika
- 3 tablespoons (45 ml) all-purpose flour
- 1 cup (235 ml) vegetable broth
- 1 28 oz. (830 ml) can crushed tomatoes
- 1 15 oz. (445 ml) can Great Northern, Navy, or Borlotti beans
- 1 cup (235 ml) shredded carrots

Instructions

1. Place the olive oil into a deep skillet and set it over medium-high heat.
2. Add the onion, garlic, salt, pepper, and paprika, and sauté it for 3-5 minutes until the onions are translucent.
3. Sit in the all-purpose flour and cook for 1-2 minutes until it is lightly toasted.
4. Add the crushed tomatoes and vegetable broth and stir until smooth.
5. Add the beans and carrots and cook for 15 minutes until the stew thickens up.
6. Serve and enjoy!

~ 67 ~

PEANUT SPINACH PESTO GNOCCHI

Pillowy clouds of gnocchi are tossed in a peanut spinach pesto and topped with crunchy roasted peanuts. This peanut spinach pesto gnocchi is simple yet oh so delicious.

Prep Time: 10 minutes| Cook Time: 10 minutes| Total Time: 20 minutes| Servings: 4

Ingredients

For the pesto:

- ½ cup (120 ml) roasted peanuts
- 2 cups (470 ml) fresh spinach
- ⅓ cup (80 ml) nutritional yeast
- ⅓ cup (80 ml) olive oil
- 1 teaspoon (5 ml) salt
- ½ teaspoon (2.5 ml) black pepper
- 2 tablespoons (30 ml) lemon juice
- 3 cloves garlic minced

For the pasta:

- 1 500 gram package (~ 4 cups/940 ml) vegan gnocchi
- ¼ cup (60 ml) roasted peanuts
- 1- 1¼ cup (235-295 ml) pesto

Instructions

1. Add the peanuts, spinach, nutritional yeast, and olive oil to a food processor's bowl and blend until it reaches your desired consistency.
2. Add the salt, pepper, lemon juice, garlic, and shallots and blend a few times until combined.
3. To prepare the gnocchi, boil the gnocchi according to the manufacturer's instructions, then drain and rinse them with cold water.
4. Place the gnocchi into a serving dish and add as much or as little peanut pesto as you like, toss to combine, then add the remaining ¼ cup of peanuts.
5. Serve and enjoy!

WHITE SPINACH MUSHROOM PINENUT LASAGNA

This white lasagna comes with a modern twist. Loaded with a homemade mozzarella creamy sauce, a spinach cream cheese spread, and sauteed mushrooms and carrots, this lasagna is creamy and delicious.

Prep Time: 15 minutes| Cook Time: 55 minutes| Total Time: 1 hour 10 minutes| Servings: 8

Ingredients

For the ricotta filling:

- 16 oz. (~2 cups/475 ml) vegan cream cheese, softened
- 10 oz. (295 ml) chopped thawed frozen spinach
- 1 cup (235 ml) vegan mozzarella cheese
- 3 tablespoons (45 ml) nutritional yeast
- ¾ cup (175 ml) toasted pine nuts
- 3 tablespoons (45 ml) freshly chopped chives

For the mushroom filling:

- 2 tablespoons (30 ml) olive oil
- ½ cup (120 ml) red onion, minced
- 3 cloves garlic, minced
- ½ cup (120 ml) red bell pepper, chopped
- 1 rib celery, diced
- 1 medium carrot, diced
- 16 oz. (2 cups/470 ml) cremini mushrooms, roughly chopped
- ½ teaspoon (2.5 ml) Italian seasoning
- ½ teaspoon (2.5 ml) salt
- ½ teaspoon (2.5 ml) black pepper

For the cheese sauce:

- 2 cups (470 ml) raw cashews
- 2 cups (470 ml) unsweetened oat milk
- 7 tablespoons (105 ml) cornstarch
- ¼ cup (60 ml) nutritional yeast
- 2 teaspoons (10 ml) apple cider vinegar
- ½ teaspoon (2.5 ml) salt
- 1 teaspoon (5 ml) garlic powder
- 1 teaspoon (5 ml) onion powder

For the lasagna:

- 1-2 boxes no-boil lasagna sheets

Instructions

1. Set your oven to 350°F (175°C) and position your oven's rack in the middle of the oven.
2. Place the soaked cashews into boiling water and allow them to soak for 20 minutes until they soften, then drain them.
3. To make the ricotta spinach filling, squeeze as much of the water as you can out of the thawed frozen spinach and place it into a bowl along with the cream cheese, mozzarella cheese, nutritional yeast, ½ cup pine nuts, and 2 tablespoons chives and stir to combine.
4. To make the mushroom filling, place the olive oil into a skillet and set it over medium-high heat.
5. Add the chopped red onions, minced garlic, and red bell peppers and cook for 3 minutes until the onions start to soften.
6. Stir in the diced celery and carrots, then cook them for 4-5 minutes until softened.
7. Add the cremini mushrooms and cook for 5-6 minutes until the onions soften and the moisture evaporates, then remove from the stove and set aside.
8. To make the cheese sauce, place the cashews, oat milk, cornstarch, nutritional yeast, apple cider vinegar, salt, garlic powder, and onion powder into a blender and blend until smooth.
9. To assemble the lasagna, add a few tablespoons of the cheese sauce to a large cast-iron skillet or baking dish and spread it into an even layer.
10. Add a layer of lasagna noodles, ⅓ of the mushroom filling, ⅓ of the cheese sauce, and ⅓ cup of the ricotta spinach filling.
11. Continue building the white mushroom spinach pine nut lasagna until only a little cheese sauce is left.
12. Top the white mushroom spinach pine nut lasagna with a final layer of noodles, then add the cheese sauce and spread the sauce into an even layer.
13. Cover the white mushroom spinach pine nut lasagna with foil, bake for 20 minutes, then remove the foil and bake for an additional 20 minutes.

14. Let the lasagna cool for 10-15 minutes, then garnish it with the remaining pine nuts and chives.
15. Serve and enjoy!

POTATO PEAR CASSEROLE

Christmas is always the perfect time for casseroles, and this potato pear casserole is no exception. This savory yet sweet casserole is seasoned with a smoky-sweet blend topped with butter and baked until golden.

Prep Time: 15 minutes| Cook Time: 45 minutes| Total Time: 1 hour| Servings: 8

Ingredients:

- 2 teaspoons (10 ml) smoked paprika
- ¼ teaspoon (1 ml) allspice
- 1 teaspoon (5 ml) salt
- ½ teaspoon (2.5 ml) black pepper
- 1 teaspoon (5 ml) garlic powder
- 1 teaspoon (5 ml) brown sugar
- 1 tablespoon (15 ml) nutritional yeast
- 8 medium potatoes, sliced into rounds
- 4 pears, peeled, cored, sliced into rounds
- ½ cup (120 ml) unsweetened coconut milk
- 3 tablespoons (45 ml) butter

Instructions

1. Turn your oven to 350°F (175°C), then spray a baking dish with non-stick cooking spray.
2. Whisk the smoked paprika, allspice, salt, black pepper, garlic powder, brown sugar, and nutritional yeast in a bowl and set it aside.
3. Arrange the potato and pear slices in a pattern in the baking dish, then sprinkle the paprika spice mixture on top of the potatoes and add the coconut milk.
4. Add the butter on top of the potato pear casserole and bake for 45 minutes to an hour until golden brown.
5. Serve and enjoy!

BUTTERNUT SQUASH CRANBERRY WELLINGTON

This festive butternut squash cranberry wellington is elegant and delicious. Loaded with butternut squash, rutabagas, cranberries, lentils, and pumpkin seeds, there is delicious flavor in every bite.

Prep Time: 10 minutes| Cook Time: 50 minutes|
Total Time: 1 hour| Servings: 6

Ingredients

- 2 tablespoons (30 ml) olive oil
- 1 small onion, diced
- 2 cloves garlic, minced
- 2 cups (470 ml) diced butternut squash
- 2 small rutabagas, diced
- 1 tablespoon (15 ml) freshly chopped tarragon
- 1 teaspoon (5 ml) sea salt
- ½ teaspoon (2.5 ml) black pepper
- 1 tablespoon (15 ml) balsamic vinegar
- 1 tablespoon (15 ml) butter
- 1 tablespoon (15 ml) red wine
- 3 tablespoons (45 ml) fine breadcrumbs
- ⅓ cup (80 ml) cranberries
- 1 ½ cups (355 ml) cooked lentils
- ⅓ cup (80 ml) pumpkin seeds
- 1 sheet vegan puff pastry
- 1 tablespoon (15 ml) unsweetened almond milk

Instructions

1. Turn your oven to 350°F (175°C), then line a cookie sheet with parchment paper.
2. Place the olive oil into a deep skillet and set it over medium-high heat.
3. Next, stir in the chopped onions and garlic and cook them for 4-5 minutes until the onions are translucent.
4. Stir in the butternut squash, rutabagas, tarragon, sea salt, black pepper, balsamic vinegar, butter, and red wine and cook it stirring every so often for 10-15 minutes until the butternut squash is tender,

5. Remove the butternut squash mixture from the stove and stir in breadcrumbs, cranberries, lentils, and pumpkin seeds, and allow to cool completely.
6. Place the puff pastry onto a floured surface, then roll it out and arrange the butternut squash mixture in a sausage shape in the center of the puff pastry.
7. Fold one end of the puff pastry over the butternut squash filling, then brush the free edge of the puff pastry with the almond milk.
8. Fold the free edge of the puff pastry over the filling, then use a fork to seal it, and fold the edges inward and seal it with a fork.
9. Arrange the butternut squash cranberry wellington on the prepared baking sheet, seam side down, and brush it with the remaining almond milk.
10. Bake the butternut squash cranberry wellington for 30 minutes until golden, then allow it to cool for 15-20 minutes before placing it on a serving dish.
11. Serve and enjoy!

DESSERTS

- Pear Walnut Cake
- Lemon Cookies
- Chocolate Strawberry Cake
- Peppermint Cupcakes
- Carrot Cake
- Chocolate OrangeTruffles
- Matcha Madeline Cookies
- Cranberry Almond Pound Cake
- Chocolate Crinkle Cookies
- Vanilla Mocha Cheese Cake
- Christmas Fruit Cake
- Cranberry Pistachio White Chocolate Bark
- Peppermint Ice cream
- White Chocolate Almond Bark
- Gingerbread Ice Cream
- Peppermint Berry Chocolate Back
- Pumpkin Pie with Whipped Cream

PEAR WALNUT CAKE

This pear walnut cake is moist and delicious. Studded with fresh pears, chopped walnuts and chocolate chips, this pear walnut cake is so good it doesn't even need frosting or a dusting of powdered sugar.

Prep Time: 15 minutes| Cook Time: 35 minutes|
Total Time: 50 minutes| Servings: 15

Ingredients

- 3 tablespoons (45 ml) ground flaxseed
- 9 tablespoons (135 ml) water
- 1 ¾ cup (410 ml) granulated sugar
- 1 cup (235 ml) canola oil
- 1 teaspoon (5 ml) vanilla extract
- 2 cups (470 ml) all-purpose flour
- 1 teaspoon (5 ml) baking soda
- 1 teaspoon (5 ml) cinnamon
- ½ teaspoon (2.5 ml) nutmeg
- ¼ teaspoon (1 ml) salt
- 5 pears peeled, cored, chopped
- 1 pear, thinly sliced
- 1 cup (235 ml) walnuts, chopped
- ½ cup (120 ml) chocolate chips

Instructions

1. Turn your oven to 350°F (175°C), then spray a 9-inch cake pan with non-stick cooking spray.
2. Whisk the flaxseed meal and water in a small bowl and set it aside for 5 minutes.
3. Add the flaxseed meal to a bowl along with the granulated sugar, canola, oil, and vanilla extract, and whisk to combine.
4. Whisk the all-purpose flour, baking soda, cinnamon, nutmeg, and salt in a separate bowl, then fold it into the flaxseed oil mixture.
5. Fold in the chopped pears, walnuts, and chocolate chips, then pour the batter into the prepared cake pan.

6. Arrange the thinly sliced pears on top of the cake and bake for 35-38 minutes until a toothpick into the cake comes out clean.
7. Allow the pear walnut cake to cool in the pan for 5 minutes, then place on a wire rack to cool completely.
8. Serve and enjoy!

LEMON COCONUT COOKIES

Lemon and coconut in cookies? What a great combination! These cookies are soft, buttery, sweet, tangy, and loaded with coconut flavor.

Prep Time: 15 minutes| Cook Time: 12 minutes|
Total Time: 27 minutes| Servings: 20

Ingredients

For the lemon cookies:

- ½ cup (120 ml) vegan Earth Balance butter
- ¾ cup (180 ml) white granulated sugar
- 2 teaspoons (10 ml) lemon extract
- 1 cup (235 ml) all-purpose flour
- 1 cup (235 ml) coconut flour
- 1 teaspoon (5 ml) baking soda
- 1 teaspoon (5 ml) baking powder
- ¼ teaspoon (1 ml) sea salt
- 1 tablespoon (15 ml) lemon zest
- 2 tablespoons (30 ml) coconut milk

For the lemon glaze:

- 1 cup (235 ml) powdered sugar
- 2 tablespoons (30 ml) freshly squeezed lemon juice

Instructions

1. Place the vegan butter and granulated sugar into a stand mixer's bowl and mix for 30 seconds to 1 minute until light and fluffy.
2. Mix in the lemon extract, then whisk the all-purpose flour, coconut flour, baking soda, and powder, and sea salt in a separate bowl, then add it to the lemon coconut cookie batter and mix until it is crumbly.
3. Add the lemon zest and coconut milk and mix the lemon coconut cookie batter thoroughly until a dough forms.
4. Turn your oven to 350°F (175°C), then line cookie sheets with parchment paper.

5. Divide the lemon coconut cookie dough into 20 round balls, place on the prepared cookie sheets, and flatten them slightly.
6. Bake the lemon coconut cookies for 12 minutes until lightly browned around the edges and let them cool completely on the tray.
7. To make the lemon coconut cookie icing, whisk the powdered sugar and lemon juice until smooth, then drizzle it over the cooled lemon coconut cookies and allow it to set.
8. Serve and enjoy!

DARK CHOCOLATE STRAWBERRY CAKE

Chocolate cake is always great at Thanksgiving or Christmas time, and this dark chocolate cake is no different. Frosted with cream chocolate buttercream and topped with strawberries, this cake is moist and delicious.

Prep Time: 20 minutes| Cook Time: 50 minutes|
Total Time: 1 hour 10 minutes| Servings: 12-14

Ingredients

For the dark chocolate cake:

- 3 cups (710 ml) all-purpose flour
- 1 cup (235 ml) granulated sugar
- ⅓ cup (80 ml) unsweetened cocoa
- 2 teaspoons (10 ml) baking soda
- 1 teaspoon (5 ml) salt
- 2 cups (470 ml) unsweetened coconut milk
- ½ cup (120 ml) canola oil
- 1 teaspoon (5 ml) vanilla extract
- 1 teaspoon (5 ml) orange liqueur

For the chocolate cream:

- ½ cup (120 ml) vegan Earth Balance butter
- ½ cup (120 ml) cocoa powder
- 3 ½ (825 ml) cups powdered sugar
- 2 tablespoons (30 ml) coconut milk
- 1 teaspoon (5 ml) vanilla extract
- 1 teaspoon (5 ml) orange liqueur
- 8 oz. (1 cup/235 ml) quartered strawberries

Instructions

1. Turn your oven to 350°F (175°C), then grease a Bundt pan.
2. Whisk the all-purpose flour, granulated sugar, cocoa powder, baking soda, and salt in a bowl.
3. Whisk the coconut milk, canola oil, vanilla extract, and orange liqueur in another bowl.

4. Combine the coconut milk mixture with the all-purpose flour.
5. Pour the dark chocolate cake batter into the prepared Bundt pan and bake for 45-50 minutes until a skewer comes out clean.
6. Let the dark chocolate cake cool in the pan for 10 minutes, then place on a wire rack to cool completely.
7. For the chocolate buttercream, place the butter, vanilla extract, and orange liqueur into a stand mixer's bowl and beat for 1 minute until creamy.
8. Add the powdered sugar and mix until smooth and creamy.
9. Frost the dark chocolate cake with the chocolate buttercream, then top it with the strawberries.
10. Serve and enjoy!

PEPPERMINT CUPCAKES

Peppermint cupcakes are the hallmark of Christmas. These peppermint cupcakes are fluffy and delicious. Topped with a pink and white peppermint frosting and candy canes, there is a taste of peppermint in every bite.

Prep Time: 20 minutes| Cook Time: 25 minutes| Total Time: 45 minutes| Servings: 12

Ingredients

For the peppermint cupcakes:

- 1 ¾ (410 ml) cups all-purpose flour
- 1 cup (235 ml) granulated sugar
- 1 teaspoon (5 ml) baking powder
- ½ teaspoon (2.5 ml) salt
- 1 cup (235 ml) coconut milk
- 1 teaspoon (5 ml) vanilla bean paste
- 1 teaspoon (5 ml) peppermint extract
- ⅓ cup (80 ml) canola oil
- 1 tablespoon (15 ml) lemon juice

For the peppermint frosting:

- ½ cup (120 ml) vegan Earth Balance butter
- 3 cups (710 ml) powdered sugar
- ½ teaspoon (2.5 ml) peppermint extract
- 2 tablespoons (30 ml) coconut milk
- 3 drops pink food coloring
- peppermint candy canes, broken into pieces

Instructions

1. Turn your oven to 350°F (175°C), then line a cupcake tin with 12 liners.
2. Whisk the all-purpose flour, granulated sugar, baking powder, and salt in a bowl.
3. Whisk the coconut milk, vanilla extract, peppermint, canola oil, and lemon juice in a bowl, then add it to the all-purpose flour mixture and stir until combined.
4. Scoop the peppermint cupcake batter into the prepared pan filling it up 3 quarters of the way, and bake for 20-25 minutes until a toothpick comes out clean.

5. Allow the peppermint cupcakes to cool in the pan for 5 minutes, then place them onto a wire rack to cool completely.
6. To make the peppermint buttercream, place the vegan butter into a stand mixer's bowl and beat for 30 seconds.
7. Add the powdered sugar, peppermint extract, and coconut milk and beat until smooth and creamy.
8. Divide the peppermint frosting between two bowls and add 3 drops of pink food coloring to one of the bowls and mix until it has a pink color.
9. Add equal portions of each frosting on opposite sides of a piping bag, frost the cupcakes, and top with the candy canes.
10. Serve and enjoy!

CARROT CAKE

Moist, rich, delicious carrot cake is studded with crunchy pecans and baked to perfection. With a sweet yet tangy frosting, this carrot cake is garnished with blueberries, pecans, sunflower seeds, and pumpkin seeds.

Prep Time: 30 minutesl Cook Time: 30 minutesl Total Time: 1 hourl Servings: 10

Ingredients

For the carrot cake:

- 2 tablespoons (30 ml) ground flaxseed meal
- 6 tablespoons (90 ml) water
- 2 cups (470 ml) all-purpose flour
- 1 teaspoon (5 ml) baking powder
- 1 teaspoon (5 ml) baking soda
- ½ teaspoon (2.5 ml) salt
- 2 teaspoons (10 ml) cinnamon
- 1 teaspoon (5 ml) nutmeg
- ½ teaspoon (2.5 ml) ginger
- ½ cup (120 ml) brown sugar
- 1 cup (235 ml) granulated brown sugar
- ½ cup (120 ml) canola oil
- 1 teaspoon (5 ml) vanilla extract
- 1 tablespoon (15 ml) lemon juice
- ½ cup (120 ml) pecans, chopped
- 2 ⅓ cups (550 ml) grated carrots

For the buttercream frosting:

- ½ cup (120 ml) vegan Earth Balance butter
- 4 cups (945 ml) powdered sugar
- 1 teaspoon (5 ml) vanilla extract
- 1 teaspoon (5 ml) lemon extract
- 2-3 tablespoons (30-45 ml) coconut milk

For the garnish:

- ¼ cup (60 ml) whole pecans
- 1 cup (235 ml) blueberries
- ¼ cup (60 ml) pumpkin seeds
- ¼ cup (60 ml) sunflower seeds

Instructions

1. Turn your oven to 350°F (175°C), then spray two 8-inch round cake pans with non-stick spray and add a parchment paper round to each pan.
2. Whisk the ground flaxseed meal and water in a bowl and let sit for 5 minutes.
3. Whisk the all-purpose flour, baking powder, baking soda, salt, cinnamon, nutmeg, and ginger in a bowl.
4. Whisk the brown sugar, granulated sugar, canola oil, vanilla extract, and lemon juice in a separate bowl until combined.
5. Add the all-purpose flour mixture to the sugar oil mixture and store to combine.
6. Fold in the shredded carrots and pecans, then divide the carrot cake batter between the prepared pans and bake the carrot cake for 30 minutes until a skewer comes out clean.
7. Let the carrot cakes cool in the pans for 5 minutes, then transfer them to a wire rack to cool completely.
8. To make the carrot cake frosting, place the vegan butter into a stand mixer's bowl and beat for 30 seconds.
9. Add the powdered sugar, vanilla extract, lemon extract, and coconut milk and beat until smooth and creamy.
10. Frost the carrot cake, then top with the pecans, blueberries, pumpkin seeds, and sunflower seeds.
11. Serve and enjoy!

CHOCOLATE ORANGE TRUFFLES

Just because you are a vegan does not mean you can't enjoy the delectably sweet flavor of truffles. These chocolate orange truffles are decadent, sweet, and oh so delicious.

Prep Time: 15 minutes| Cook Time: 0 minutes|
Total Time: 15 minutes| Servings: 14

Ingredients

- 10 Medjool dates
- ½ cup (120 ml) pecans
- ½ cup (120 ml) almonds
- ¼ cup + ¼ cup cocoa powder for rolling (½ cup total/120 ml)
- 1 tablespoon (15 ml) cashew butter
- 1 tablespoon (15 ml) maple syrup
- 2 tablespoons (30 ml) freshly squeezed orange juice
- zest of 1 orange
- 1-2 tablespoons (15-30 ml) all-purpose flour

Instructions

1. Place the Medjool dates in a food processor bowl along with the pecans and almonds and pulse on high for 30 seconds until it develops a sandy texture.
2. Add ¼ cup cocoa powder, maple syrup, orange juice, orange zest, and a tablespoon of flour and pulse until a smooth dough forms, adding in the remaining tablespoon of all-purpose flour if necessary.
3. Roll the chocolate orange balls into 14, 1-inch balls, then roll them in the remaining cocoa powder.
4. Serve and enjoy!

MATCHA MADELEINES

Traditional French Madeleines get a dose of Matcha flavor. Reminiscent of a sponge cake, these French cookies are soft and delicious with the perfect amount of sweetness.

Prep Time: 15 minutes| Chill time: 3 hours|
Cook Time: 13 minutes|
Total Time: 3 hours, 28 minutes| Servings: 18-24

Ingredients

- 2 tablespoons (30 ml) flaxseed meal
- 1 cup (235 ml) all-purpose flour
- ½ cup (120 ml) coconut milk
- ½ cup + 1 tablespoon (135 ml) vegan earth balance butter, melted
- ½ cup (120 ml) granulated sugar
- 1 cup + 1 tablespoon (250 ml) butter
- ¼ teaspoon (1 ml) salt
- 1 teaspoon (5 ml) baking powder
- 2 tablespoons (30 ml) matcha powder
- 1 teaspoon (5 ml) vanilla extract
- 1 tablespoon (15 ml) powdered sugar

Instructions

1. Whisk the ground flaxseed meal and coconut milk in a bowl and set aside for 15 minutes.
2. Place the granulated sugar in a bowl, then place a sieve on top of the bowl and sift in the 1 cup of all-purpose flour, salt, baking powder, and matcha powder; remove the sieve and whisk to combine.
3. Add the vanilla extract to the flaxseed meal and coconut milk mixture and stir to combine.
4. Add the vanilla flaxseed mixture to the matcha Madeleine batter and gently stir to combine.
5. Gradually, stir in ¼ cup of melted butter, then add the remaining ¼ cup of melted butter and stir to combine and cover the matcha Madeleine batter with plastic wrap and chill the batter for 3 hours or overnight.

6. Place your oven's rack into the center of the oven and turn it to 375°F (190°C).
7. Brush 2, 12-hole Madeleine shell shape pans with the tablespoon of melted butter and dust it with 1 tablespoon (15 ml) of all-purpose flour.
8. Remove the matcha Madeleine batter from the fridge and fill each shell with 1 tablespoon of the batter.
9. Bake the matcha Madeleines for 11-13 minutes until the edges are golden.
10. Allow the matcha Madeleines to cool in the shell for 3 minutes, then use a fork to carefully remove them from the Madeleine pan and place them on a wire rack to cool completely.
11. Dust the matcha Madeleines with the powdered sugar.
12. Serve and enjoy!

CRANBERRY ALMOND POUND CAKE

Pound cake is necessary at Christmas time. Featuring tart, sweet cranberries, this cake is rich, moist, and delicious.

Prep Time: 20 minutes| Cook Time: 50 minutes| Total Time: 1 hour 10 minutes| Servings: 10

Ingredients

- 1 cup (235 ml) all-purpose flour
- 1 cup (235 ml) finely ground almond flour
- 1 tablespoon (15 ml) baking powder
- ½ teaspoon (2.5 ml) salt
- 2 tablespoons (30 ml) coconut oil, melted
- 1 tablespoon (15 ml) orange juice
- ½ cup (120 ml) vegan Earth Balance butter
- 1 cup (235 ml) granulated sugar
- 1 tablespoon (15 ml) finely grated orange zest
- 1 cup (235 ml) vegan sour cream
- ⅓ cup (80 ml) cranberries

Instructions

1. Place your oven's rack into the center of the oven and turn it to 350°F (175°C).
2. Spray an 8 x 9-inch loaf pan with non-stick cooking spray.
3. Mix together the all-purpose flour, almond flour baking powder, and salt in a bowl, then set aside.
4. Whisk the coconut oil and orange juice in a bowl, then set it aside.
5. Place the vegan butter, granulated sugar, and orange zest into a stand mixer's bowl and beat it until light and fluffy.
6. Add the vegan sour cream and mix to combine, scraping the bowl as needed.
7. Add the all-purpose flour almond mixture in thirds, alternating with the coconut oil and lemon juice, and mix until combined.

8. Fold in the cranberries, then pour cake batter into the prepared pan and bake for 50-55 minutes.
9. Let the cake cool for 5 minutes in the pan, then carefully unmold it and place it onto a wire rack to cool completely.
10. Serve and enjoy!

CHOCOLATE CRINKLE COOKIES

Chocolate crinkle cookies are rich, tasty, and fudgy. In addition to this, they are also irresistibly stunning. These classic Christmas cookies are a delicious crowd-pleaser.

Prep Time: 20 minutes| Cook Time: 10 minutes| Total Time: 30 minutes| Servings: 18

Ingredients

- 1 cup (235 ml) granulated sugar
- ⅓ cup (80 ml) canola oil
- 1 tablespoon (15 ml) ground flaxseed meal
- ⅓ cup (80 ml) coconut milk
- 1 teaspoon (5 ml) pure vanilla bean paste
- 1 ¼ cups (295 ml) all-purpose flour
- 1 teaspoon (5 ml) cinnamon
- ½ cup (120 ml) cocoa powder
- 1 teaspoon (5 ml) baking powder
- ¼ teaspoon (1 ml) salt
- 1 cup (235 ml) powdered sugar

Instructions

1. Turn oven to 350°F (175°C), then line 2 cookie sheets with parchment paper.
2. Whisk the granulated sugar and canola oil in a bowl until combined, then stir in the flaxseeds, coconut milk, and vanilla bean paste.
3. Place the all-purpose flour, cocoa powder, baking powder, salt, and cinnamon in a bowl and mix until combined, then stir it into the sugar oil mixture until a dough forms.
4. Place the powdered sugar into a shallow baking dish, divide the chocolate crinkle dough into 18 balls, and roll each cookie into the powdered sugar.
5. Place the cookies onto the prepared pan leaving 2-inches of space between each cookie, and bake for 10-12 minutes.
6. Let the cookies cool on the pan for 10 minutes, then place them on a wire rack to cool completely.
7. Serve and enjoy!

VANILLA MOCHA CHEESECAKE

This silky smooth vanilla mocha cheesecake is truly divine. Featuring a walnut date crust, this cheesecake is smooth, creamy, and delicious — best of all, this cheesecake is gluten-free.

Prep Time: 20 minutes| Chill time: 4 hours|
Cook Time: 10 minutes|
Total Time: 4 hours, 30 minutes| Servings: 10 Slices

Ingredients

For the nut crust:

- 6 Medjool dates
- 6 graham crackers, broken into pieces
- 3 tablespoons (45 ml) melted vegan butter
- ½ cup (120 ml) walnuts

For the cheesecake:

- 16 oz. (470 ml) vegan cream cheese, room temperature
- ⅔ cup (160 ml) granulated sugar
- 2 tablespoons (30 ml) tapioca starch
- 3 tablespoon (45 ml) coconut milk
- 1 tablespoon (15 ml) lemon juice
- 1 tablespoon (15 ml) vanilla bean paste
- 1 tablespoon (15 ml) mocha frappe powder
- 8 oz. (1 cup/235 ml) blueberries or blackberries

Instructions

1. Place the Medjool dates, graham crackers, butter, and walnuts into a food processor's bowl and blend until coarse but not completely smooth.
2. Press the nut crust into an 8-inch spring-form pan greased with non-stick baking spray and set aside.
3. Turn your oven to 350°F (175°C).
4. Place the vegan cream cheese and granulated sugar into a stand mixer's bowl and mix on low until the sugar dissolves and it is smooth and creamy.

5. With the stand mixer running, add the tapioca starch, coconut milk, lemon juice, vanilla bean paste, and mocha frappe powder and mix until combined.
6. Increase the mixer's speed to high and beat for 2 minutes until smooth.
7. Pour the vanilla mocha cheesecake into the prepared pan and bake for 40-45 minutes.
8. Allow the vanilla mocha cheesecake to cool completely, then refrigerate overnight for 4 hours or overnight.
9. Top the vanilla mocha cheesecake with the blueberries or blackberries.
10. Serve and enjoy!

CHRISTMAS FRUIT CAKE

There is no Christmas without fruit cake. This fruit cake is moist, rich, and filled with rum-soaked raisins, sultanas, currants, and dried cranberries. This fruit cake is the perfect way to bring your Christmas dinner to a close.

Prep Time: 20 minutes| Cook Time: 3 hours|
Soaking Time: 12 hours|
Total Time: 3 hours 20 minutes|
Servings: 12 people

Ingredients

- ½ cup (120 ml) golden raisins
- ½ cup (120 ml) sultanas
- ½ cup (120 ml) currants
- ⅓ cup (80 ml) dried cranberries
- ¼ cup (60 ml) candied orange peel, diced
- 6 tablespoons + 1 teaspoon (95 ml) dark rum
- ⅔ cup (160 ml) vegan Earth Balance butter
- ⅔ cup (160 ml) dark brown sugar
- ⅓ cup (80 ml) granulated sugar
- 1 tablespoon (15 ml) molasses
- zest of 1 lemon
- 3 cups (710 ml) all-purpose flour
- ⅓ cup (80 ml) finely ground almond flour
- ¾ teaspoon (4 ml) baking soda
- 1 teaspoon (5 ml) cinnamon
- ½ teaspoon (2.5 ml) nutmeg
- ½ teaspoon (2.5 ml) ginger
- ½ teaspoon (2.5 ml) cardamom
- ½ cup (120 ml) coconut milk
- 2 tablespoons (30 ml) apple cider vinegar
- 2 oz. (60 ml) walnuts, chopped

Instructions

1. Combine the golden raisins, sultanas, currants, cranberries, and rum in a bowl, cover with plastic wrap and let sit overnight.

2. Turn your oven to 350°F (175°C), then line 2, 8 by 9-inch loaf pans with a double layer of parchment paper.
3. Add the vegan butter, brown sugar, granulated sugar, molasses, and lemon zest in a stand mixer's bowl and beat the mixture until light and fluffy.
4. Whisk the all-purpose flour, almond flour, baking soda, cinnamon, nutmeg, cloves, and cardamom in a bowl.
5. Add the all-purpose flour almond mixture to the butter mixture along with the coconut milk and apple cider vinegar, just until combined. The fruit cake batter should be thick.
6. Fold in the soaked fruits along with the liquid and chopped walnuts.
7. Divide the fruit cake batter between the prepared loaf pans and bake for 2-3 hours until a skewer comes out clean.
8. Allow the fruit cake to cool completely, add more rum if desired.
9. Serve and enjoy!

CRANBERRY PISTACHIO WHITE CHOCOLATE BARK

Featuring tart-sweet dried cranberries, slightly sweet, nutty pistachios, and decadent, silky smooth white chocolate, this cranberry pistachio white chocolate bark is elegant and so darn delicious.

Prep Time: 15 minutes| Cook Time: 5 minutes| Total Time: 20 minutes| Servings: 12

Ingredients

- 1 ⅓ cups (315 ml) non-dairy white chocolate chips
- 2 teaspoons (10 ml) coconut oil
- 1 teaspoon (5 ml) vanilla extract
- ¼ teaspoon (1 ml) sea salt
- ½ cup (120 ml) cranberries
- 1 cup (235 ml) roasted pistachios

Instructions

1. Line a cookie sheet with parchment paper and set aside.
2. Place the chocolate chips and coconut oil into a pot and set over low heat.
3. Stir the white chocolate chips frequently until melted, then pour onto a parchment-lined cookie sheet and spread it into an even layer.
4. Top with the cranberries and pistachios and allow the white chocolate bark to sit for 15 minutes until hardened, then break into pieces.
5. Serve and enjoy!

PEPPERMINT ICE CREAM

This peppermint ice cream is creamy and dreamy. Studded with crushed candy canes and sweetened with maple syrup, one scoop of this peppermint ice cream is simply not enough.

Prep Time: 5 minutes| Cook Time: 0 hours|
Freezing Time: 4 hours|
Total Time: 4 hours 5 minutes| Servings: 6 people

Ingredients

- 1 15 oz. (445 ml) can full-fat coconut milk
- 1 cup (235 ml) cashew milk
- 1 tablespoon (15 ml) tapioca starch
- ¼ cup (60 ml) maple syrup
- 1 teaspoon (5 ml) peppermint extract
- 1 teaspoon (5 ml) vanilla bean paste
- 4 peppermint candy canes, crushed

Instructions

1. Add the coconut milk, cashew milk, tapioca starch, maple syrup, peppermint extract, and vanilla bean paste into a blender and blend until combined.
2. Pour the peppermint ice cream batter into a bowl, cover with plastic wrap and refrigerate it overnight.
3. Churn the peppermint ice cream in an ice cream maker according to the manufacturer's instructions.
4. Fold in the peppermint crushed candy cane pieces during the last 5 minutes of churning time.
5. Place the peppermint ice cream into a freezer-safe airtight container and freeze for 3-4 hours until firm.
6. Serve and enjoy!

GINGERBREAD ICE CREAM

With a coconut cashew base, spices such as cinnamon, nutmeg, and ginger, and chunks of gingerbread cookies, this gingerbread ice cream is ever so creamy and plain old delicious.

Prep Time: 15 minutes| Cook Time: 0 hours|
Freezing Time: 4 hours|
Total Time: 4 hours 15 minutes| Servings: 6 people

Ingredients

- 1 15 oz. (445 ml) can full-fat coconut milk
- 1 cup (235 ml) cashew milk
- 1 tablespoon (15 ml) tapioca starch
- ¼ cup (60 ml) maple syrup
- 1 teaspoon (5 ml) cinnamon
- ½ teaspoon (2.5 ml) nutmeg
- 1 teaspoon (5 ml) ginger
- 6 vegan gingerbread cookies, crushed

Instructions

1. Add the coconut milk, cashew milk, tapioca starch, maple syrup, cinnamon, nutmeg, and ginger into a blender and blend until combined.
2. Pour the gingerbread ice cream batter into a bowl, cover with plastic wrap and refrigerate overnight.
3. Churn the gingerbread ice cream in an ice cream maker according to the manufacturer's instructions.
4. Fold in the crushed gingerbread cookies during the last 5 minutes of churning time.
5. Place the gingerbread ice cream into a freezer-safe airtight container and freeze for 3-4 hours until firm.
6. Serve and enjoy!

PEPPERMINT BERRY CHOCOLATE BARK

This peppermint berry chocolate bark is elegant and delicious. With crunchy almonds and crushed freeze-dried berries, this chocolate bark is rich and tasty.

Prep Time: 15 minutes| Chill Time: 1 hour|
Total Time: 1 hour 15 minutes| Servings: 12

Ingredients

- 3 cups (710 ml) vegan chocolate chips
- 1 cup (235 ml) crushed freeze-dried berries
- 1 cup (235 ml) crushed almonds
- 10 candy canes broken into pieces

Instructions

1. Place the vegan chocolate chips into a microwave-safe bowl and microwave it in 30-second bursts until smooth and melted.
2. Pour the melted chocolate chips onto a parchment-lined cookie sheet and spread into an even layer.
3. Top with the freeze-dried berries, almonds, and candy canes and chill for 1 hour until set.
4. Break the peppermint berry chocolate bark into pieces.
5. Serve and enjoy!

PUMPKIN PIE

Pumpkin Pie is a staple for most Thanksgiving and even Christmas dinners! This classic recipe will be eaten up before you know it!

Prep Time: 30 minutes| Chill time: 4 hours|
Cook Time: 1 hour| Total Time: 5 hours 30 minutes|
Servings: 8-12

Ingredients

For the crust:

- 1 ½ cups (355 ml) all purpose flour, spooned and levelled
- ¼ teaspoon (1 ml) salt
- ¼ cup (60 ml) Earth Balance vegan butter, cold and cut into cubes
- ¼ cup (60 ml) vegetable shortening, cold and cut into pieces
- 3-4 tablespoons (45-60 ml) ice water

For the filling:

- 1 15 ounce (445 ml) can pumpkin puree
- ½ cup (120 ml) soy, almond or rice milk
- ¼ cup (60 ml) maple syrup
- ½ cup (235 ml) brown sugar
- 1 teaspoon (5 ml) cinnamon
- 1 teaspoon (5 ml) ginger
- ½ teaspoon (2.5 ml) nutmeg
- ⅛ teaspoon (.6 ml) cloves
- ½ teaspoon (2.5 ml) salt
- 3 tablespoons (45 ml) cornstarch

For the whipped cream

- 1 14-ounce (415 ml) can coconut cream or full fat coconut milk
- ½ cup (120 ml) icing/powdered sugar
- ½ teaspoon (2.5 ml) vanilla extract

Instructions

For the crust

1. Mix together the dry ingredients in a large bowl, then add the cold butter and shortening. Use a pastry cutter or fork to cut it in, then drizzle in the ice water and stir until the dough comes together.
2. Dump the dough onto a lightly floured surface and shape into a ball.
3. Roll the dough with a rolling pin to about a 12-inch circle, and transfer to a 9-inch pie plate.
4. Gently push the pie crust all around the dish, trimming off any excess and fixing any spots that need repair.
5. Use immediately or refrigerate. Double the recipe for 2 pie crusts (top and bottom).

For the filling

1. Add the canned pumpkin, milk, brown sugar, maple syrup, cinnamon, ginger, nutmeg, cloves, salt and cornstarch to a blender and blend until very smooth. You may also simply whisk it together in a bowl until smooth.
2. Pour the mixture into the pie crust and spread with a spatula.
3. Bake for 1 hour. Cool at room temperature and refrigerate for at least 4 hours or overnight.

For the whipped cream:

1. Chill coconut cream overnight in the can, in the morning scrape of the hardened top layer and place in a chilled mixing bow.
2. Beat with a mixer for 30 seconds, add in powdered sugar and vanilla. Beat 1 more minute. Do not over whip.
3. Serve immediately or keep in the fridge for up to 2 weeks!

CONCLUSION

The Holiday season is about spending quality time with the ones we love and eating delicious food. Although, a vegan Christmas or Thanksgiving dinner can be a bit challenging. There's no need to dread the Holidays anymore as you now have over 50 brand new original recipes in your arsenal to share with others.

At the end of the day, Christmas and Thanksgiving are not about ham, turkey, brussel sprouts, butternut squash, cranberry Wellington, or vegan meatloaf. It's about spending time with the ones you love. In the spirit of helping each other out, you could offer to bring a few vegan dishes so that everyone can partake in them and understand that being vegan is much more than just eating salad or vegetables. By the time next year rolls around, you will have turned into a confident vegan chef. Remember, everyone encounters a few hiccups in the kitchen, especially when you are hosting dinner, but be sure to take time to enjoy yourself during the Holidays! Happy Cooking!

Printed in Great Britain
by Amazon